Outsourcing–Insourcing

Outsourcing–Insourcing

Can vendors make money from the new relationship opportunities?

**Per Jenster, Henrik Stener Pedersen,
Patricia Plackett and David Hussey**

John Wiley & Sons, Ltd

Copyright © 2005   John Wiley & Sons Ltd, The Atrium, Southern Gate, Chichester,
West Sussex PO19 8SQ, England

Telephone   (+44) 1243 779777

Email (for orders and customer service enquiries): cs-books@wiley.co.uk
Visit our Home Page on www.wiley.com

Other Wiley Editorial Offices

John Wiley & Sons Inc., 111 River Street, Hoboken, NJ 07030, USA

Jossey-Bass, 989 Market Street, San Francisco, CA 94103-1741, USA

Wiley-VCH Verlag GmbH, Boschstr. 12, D-69469 Weinheim, Germany

John Wiley & Sons Australia Ltd, 33 Park Road, Milton, Queensland 4064, Australia

John Wiley & Sons (Asia) Pte Ltd, 2 Clementi Loop #02-01, Jin Xing Distripark,
Singapore 129809

John Wiley & Sons Canada Ltd, 22 Worcester Road, Etobicoke, Ontario, Canada M9W 1L1

Wiley also publishes its books in a variety of electronic formats. Some content that appears
in print may not be available in electronic books.

Library of Congress Cataloguing-in-Publication Data

Outsourcing–insourcing : can vendors make money from the new relationship
  opportunities? / Per Jenster, Henrik Stener Pedersen, Patricia Plackett and David Hussey.
      p.   cm.
    Includes index.
    ISBN 0-470-84490-6 (alk. paper)
    1. Contracting out.   2. Industrial procurement.   I. Jenster, Per V.
  HD2365.O9435   2005
  658 .7′23—dc22   2004025691

British Library Cataloguing in Publication Data

A catalogue record for this book is available from the British Library

ISBN 0-470-84490-6 (hb)

Typeset in 11/16pt Garamond by TechBooks, New Delhi, India
Printed and bound in Great Britain by Antony Rowe Ltd, Chippenham, Wiltshire
This book is printed on acid-free paper responsibly manufactured from sustainable forestry
in which at least two trees are planted for each one used for paper production.

Contents

Preface

Outsourcing started to become fashionable in the late 1980s. However, it very much came of age in the 1990s, and certainly became a normal part of corporate life by the turn of the century. It is built on three long-established principles – corporate focus on core competencies, 'make or buy' make or buy cost analysis and the preferred supplier concepts of total quality management. And now global outsourcing is on everyone's mind.

Initially much of outsourcing was at the easily definable end of the spectrum – such as having a supplier make a component previously manufactured in-house, taking over management of the company cafeteria, or using a fleet of rented trucks for services previously carried out internally. Such activities remain a part of the outsourcing spectrum today, but the big opportunities for suppliers lie at the other end of the spectrum where suppliers become strategic partners of the organization for a specific, but not always easy-to-define, slate of activities that might, for example, add product improvement and development to the supply of a subassembly for which not even the components were previously bought outside the firm. It is not uncommon now for entire departments such as accounting and R&D to be fully outsourced.

Questions of relevance for outsourcing activities at the strategic partnering end of the spectrum include the following:

- What form of relationship or strategic alliance should be established between the buyer of outsourced services and the seller of those services?
- What are the scope, scale and importance of the outsourced activities?
- What pricing strategy should be used and what risk-sharing is involved?
- What are the changes to organizations that lead to decisions to seek more service outsourcing?

The literature on outsourcing has grown rapidly, and there is an increasing number of books on this subject. Much of the work on outsourcing has taken the perspective of the buying organization, and the specific strategic and operational difficulties that buyers face. However, there are at least two organizations in every outsourcing decision: What, for the buying organization, is a strategic decision involving benefits, risks and organizational change, is for the selling organization a strategic opportunity, which has a related, but different, series of benefits, risks and organizational implications. Unlike the majority of publications on outsourcing this book takes the perspective of the seller of outsourcing services specifically in terms of outsourcing strategy and implementation. In so doing, this book fills a gap in the business studies literature.

Today, one can hardly open a newspaper or switch on the television before the topic of global outsourcing appears; however, the issues are more concerned with the international trade aspects of outsourcing. It is less the business aspects and more the outsourcing of jobs that raises eyebrows. The themes of this book are less concerned about this 'flavour of the month', as the concerns about vanishing jobs to overseas vendors have been around for centuries. What this book does focus on are the firm-specific business aspects of outsourcing and the complexities being imposed as firms engage in new business areas focusing on delivering complex business solutions.

The foundation of this book is three years of research activity at Copenhagen Business School, funded by the school and the Danish Industrial Mortgage Foundation, as well as the Confederation of Danish Industry. The research project included the participation of 12 companies that provided active participation and funding for the research. The firms and their industries are listed below:

- Diversey-Lever   cleaning system
- Berendsen Textil A/S   textile management
- Berendsen PMC A/S   compression technology
- Bossard Group   fasteners
- NEG-Mikron A/S   windmills
- PostDanmark   transport systems
- BP/Mobile/Exxon   lubricants
- Quest International   flavour systems
- IBM Danmark   information technologies
- Sjællandske Kraftværker   utility management
- Oxford Research   business research services
- Canon   office equipment

Most of the participating companies are international, if not global, players in their respective industries. One area of focus was the transition from the provision of a narrowly defined product and service portfolio to a dramatic shift in scale to more complex solutions. The combination of research on the companies studied as well as case studies and the study of participant contributions has provided a much fuller picture of outsourcing from the supplier side.

The research project was organized around a number of PhD studies, clinical studies of specific companies and issues, surveys, literature reviews, research colloquiums, management workshops and a large international conference. The contributing researchers, apart from the authors of this book, included Mikael Lynnerup, Michael Ahern, Kim Møller, Mogens Bjerre, Jens Geersbro, Trine Erdal, Carlos Cordon (IMD professor) and Tom Vollmann (IMD professor) – we thank them all for their valuable contribution.

For managers at various levels in organizations who are already involved in outsourcing, or who see the need to become involved in supplying value-added outsourcing products and services, this book offers a range of practical management insights. We feel that the book is particularly valuable for those who currently offer outsourcing services but who have not as yet moved to the strategic partnering end of the outsourcing spectrum. For participants in MBA programmes and in executive management courses this book offers comprehensive coverage of a topic of increasing relevance in this era of ever-increasing economic globalization.

Finally, we would like to make a special tribute to David Hussey, a close friend and colleague and a significant contributor to business literature over many years, who died in January 2003.

Introduction

If you are competing with the rest of the world, you had better focus on what you are good at.

Focusing on what you are good at in companies today means a careful assessment of core competencies within a broader industrial context and strategically outsourcing many other activities. Companies are being transformed from highly integrated organizations producing and delivering goods and services themselves to much more specialized enterprises that contract out to the marketplace for many goods and services. As a consequence, successful outsourcing has become a key to competitiveness. Because the new relationship opportunities for profitable business outsourcing are global in nature, cross-cultural management issues are increasingly a factor that adds to the complexity of the task.

In this book we examine the key issues of relevance to successful outsourcing. Our focus is on profitable business strategies. A diverse range of examples is used to illustrate the key features of outsourcing success and failure.

Overview of key issues in this book

Each chapter addresses a specific aspect that is required for successfully managing the supply of outsourcing services taking buyer perspectives into account:

1. *Understanding the opportunities*: Understanding what is driving customers. The changes taking place in purchasing organizations. The supplier view of the impact of what is happening. The spectrum of outsourcing arrangements that is possible.

2. *Moving to supplying a total solution*: Strategic and organizational implications. The issues that have to be considered. Lessons learned from companies that have managed the transition to total solution provision.

3. *Retooling marketing and the sales force*: Market segment identification. New ways of market segmentation (e.g., by customer strategy). Mining the segment. Positioning the offer. Selling solutions. Different requirements of the sales force. Managing and motivating the sales force. Changing competency requirements.

4. *Managing buyer/supplier relationships*: Organizational changes in both parties. Cultural shifts. Communication issues. Information sharing.

5. *Pricing solutions and managing risks*: Pricing strategies for solutions. Understanding the risks to both suppliers and buyers and creating appropriate pricing. Avoiding risks.

6. *'Transitioning' human resources*: Implications for employees. Where competencies change. Training, recruitment, reward and retention issues. Temporary employees.

7. *Structuring 'next generation' IT solutions*: Aligning systems with the customers. Ensuring that systems give the strategic and control information needed for the new arrangements. Where information may add value.

8. *Achieving quality in outsourcing*: Meeting quality requirements. Cooperating with customers and other vendors. Philosophy of continual improvement.

9. *Getting a good slice of a larger pie*: Working with buyers to make the overall pie larger. Getting a larger slice of the pie from seller and buyer perspectives. Enhancing outsourcing profitability.

Understanding the opportunities

Introduction

Outsourcing – that is, the process of shifting tasks and services previously performed in-house to outside vendors – is hardly a new idea in management. But the volume, extent and character of outsourcing have been changing rapidly. The challenges are not merely simple 'make or buy' decisions, but also responses to what some have declared as the new round of globalization in which not only typical manufacturing jobs are being sent offshore, but also upscale tasks, such as research projects, technical service support functions, engineering and even financial analysis, are being placed in so-called developing countries. In this chapter we look at the historical development of outsourcing and current trends. We also introduce our classification system for four key types of outsourcing activities. The decision drivers for each are presented both from the perspective of the seller of the outsourced solution and from the perspective of the buyer of the solution.

What is outsourcing?

Outsourcing is now high on the list of the things that many savants believe well-run organizations must consider, so that it is now as much a management fad as a reasoned decision, offering important augmentation to the current organizational design, or even giving rise to new enterprise designs. It can offer great opportunities to both the buyer and supplier when used wisely. However, when it becomes a mantra, used without thought, it can do great damage to both parties.

According to the *Wall Street Journal*, Indian labour in banking costs about one-tenth as much as comparable banking personnel in Europe and the U.S. However, employing someone in back office processing in India is only about 50% less expensive once other costs are factored in. Wages in India are also rising rapidly each year, a factor that could make the savings short-lived.[1]

What is outsourcing? One definition is *the market procurement of formerly in-house produced goods and services from legally independent supplier firms* (Semlinger, 1991). Like all definitions, it gives the scope of the topic but conceals the infinite variety of outsourcing possibilities. It makes it clear that there are two parties to an outsourcing arrangement, but is really a definition from the buyer viewpoint. The supplier may have decisions to make that are as tough as any faced by the organization taking a decision to outsource. In fact, outsourcing can be an opportunity for both parties, but it may also do damage to one or both of the parties. We hope that we can show in this book some of the pitfalls and the principles on which good outsourcing decisions should be taken, and also look at the issue from the viewpoint of both parties.

The origins of outsourcing

Because outsourcing has gained much in popularity, it is tempting to think of it as new. Certainly it has changed shape and may have a different form today, but the concept is centuries old. It is another form of what economists call specialization, which has been defined

---

[1] *Wall Street Journal*, 29 March, 2004.

as *concentrating activity in those lines of production in which the individual or firm has some natural or acquired advantage* (Pearce, 1983).

Imagine a primitive village of several thousand years BC in which every family made its own pots, spears and arrows, and hunted and gathered its own food. Since some people were naturally more skilled at certain of these tasks than others, they began to concentrate on their core competencies (to borrow a phrase from Prahalad and Hamel, 1990), such as weapon making, and to outsource the other things that they used to do, such as hunting. They bartered their knives, spears and arrows for the things they no longer produced. Later money became the medium of exchange, but the principles of modern outsourcing can be said to have had their roots in the recognition that there were economic benefits in specialization.

Hamel and Prahalad (1994, p. 219) state that a core competence is *a bundle of skills and technologies that enables a company to provide a particular benefit to customers.* Although the technology of making flint-headed weapons is basic, the skill level is high. (Try making some, if you do not believe us.) Flints have to be found, selected, knapped, and the resultant blades and heads fixed to a haft or shaft, which also required skill to make. The benefits of specialization were in the increased quantity and quality of all the needs of the village that could be gained if people concentrated on doing the tasks for which they were most skilled.

But there was another benefit. The 'learning curve effect' meant that the amount of time needed to produce a product would have diminished as more experience was gained. This effect meant that more thinking time could be freed up with the result that ideas could be developed for improving the product and the processes by which it was made.

Put another way, there was an opportunity cost when every family tried to be self-sufficient in all respects. As long as people had to spend a disproportionate amount of time on the things they were not good at, they could not spend that time on tasks for which they had comparative advantages. So, without specialization the overall output and quality of what was produced would have been lower, as would the rate of innovation. Although our primitive prehistoric villagers would not have understood terms like core competencies, outsourcing, productivity increases, opportunity cost, or learning curves, the benefits were real and it is these that lie at the heart of many of the modern arguments in favour of outsourcing. However, our basic example shows something that is often overlooked today: there have to be benefits for suppliers as well as for buyers.

Modern organizations are nurtured by another outgrowth from the specialization roots – division of labour – which means that the modern organization consists of individuals who have different skills, attributes and competencies, and who are hired to fulfil a specific task or role. Few organizations of the last century or so have attempted to do everything themselves. There were always some products and services that came from outside suppliers and were never made in-house, and the boundaries between the two were flexible. The main manifestation of outsourcing until the early 1980s was the 'make or buy' decision. The focus of this activity was mainly on cost reduction, and the main writing about this topic that we have seen is in books on accounting. This quote from Anthony and Reece (1978, p. 672) is typical of what has appeared in accounting books before and since 1978:

> *Make or buy*. Make or buy decisions are among the most com-
> mon type of alternative choice problems. At any given time, an
> organisation performs certain activities with its own resources,
> and it pays outside firms to perform certain other activities. It
> constantly seeks to improve the balance between the two types
> of activities by asking: should we contract with some outside

party to perform some function that we are now performing ourselves? Or should we perform some activity that we now pay someone else to do?

Although in practice both opportunity cost and strategic implications were usually taken into account in the final decision, up until the early 1980s most 'make or buy' decisions were cost-driven. Although some services had been outsourced by this time, more frequently outsourcing decisions applied to components. There were already well-established specialist organizations providing in-house catering and security services, so the concept of suppliers whose main mission was to perform this type of work existed long before the outsourcing of services became more common. At least one modern book (e.g., Nohria, 1998, p. 276) appears stuck with the erroneous idea that outsourcing is a 'make or buy' decision about components and not about services:

Outsourcing. The purchase of parts from outside suppliers. Many American small appliance manufacturers use a great deal of outsourcing. The various parts and subassemblies for, say, a toaster or a blender are manufactured by a number of different companies, the so-called manufacturer does only the assembly and selling. When a company is heavily outsourced it is referred to as 'hollow.' Outsourcing is usually a good idea if the outsource can provide the parts or components at lower cost or higher quality. Outsourcing is an economic decision.

Starting in the 1980s services became a target for outsourcing. One stimulus to this change in the UK, which overflowed into other countries, was the move to privatize many of the organizations in the public sector. An early manifestation of this trend was the requirement for local authorities to market test many of the activities that they ran by having the current departments doing the job tender on the same basis as external suppliers. In many areas this led to the outsourcing of some traditional local authority activities such as refuse collection, school meal services, and the repair of council owned houses. In Denmark, for example, local authorities were pushed to bid on tenders covering activities on an equal footing with private firms in order to ensure 'best service at lowest costs'.

This activity helped create an awareness that all organizations contained a myriad of service activities and that it was possible to outsource a number of these. The scene was then set for the modern phase in outsourcing activity. However, this phase was triggered by a number of trends and pressures that provided the incentive to change the thinking behind outsourcing and to take it in new directions. Before we explore the new directions we should look at some of the triggers that have caused the explosion in outsourcing activity.

Trends and pressures

Many of the trends and pressures have been with us since the 1980s, although the form of some of them has changed. Traditional concepts of management have been challenged and re-examined against the challenge of these external changes and the way they are expected to develop in the future. The pace of change has been a feature of the modern world for many decades, and may not be much more turbulent today than it was in the past – it only seems so because we are dealing directly with the forces for change. However, there are two features that are different: there is no 'hiding place' in that these forces for change have no geographical boundaries and few organizations and few countries are immune to them. Furthermore, the potential impact of change on economic performance is probably greater than in the past.

There is also a cumulative impact from the combination of all the megatrends because they are occurring simultaneously:

- *Competition/globalization is increasing.* Competition has increased and for most industries it is no longer possible to define competition within the boundaries of a particular industry or country. There has been a steady blurring of industry boundaries since the mid-1970s and many once-distinct industries have grown closer together. Technological advances have meant that computers, cameras, video, typewriters, copiers and telephones have all crossed into each other's territories, bringing new competitors and product obsolescence. Many artificial boundaries have disappeared in the professional services industries. More and more organizations are compelled to think of their businesses in global terms, either because their customers demand a global orientation because they themselves are global, or because it has become impossible to achieve the volumes to match competitors' costs without serving a larger market area. Few businesses have escaped the ever-increasing intensities of competition. The twist given in the new millennium has been e-business, which has created new competitors and new ways to compete.
- *Customers are more demanding.* The lifestyle expectations of the whole population have increased steadily and they continue to rise. Many in the developed countries regard poverty as relative, rather than absolute, deprivation. With higher expectations, and more choice, it is not surprising that the individual consumer is less tolerant of poor products and service and is more vocal in expressing dissatisfaction. The industrial customer is more demanding, quite rightly so, in order to attain the cost levels and to supply the quality and timeliness of delivery that enable him/her to compete. Although the new requirements bring opportunities

for the whole supply chain to work in a more cooperative manner than may have been traditional, there is much less willingness by industrial customers to condone failures. Few can afford to do so, if they are to succeed in their own markets.

Customers who have embraced outsourcing as one of their responses to change today have vastly different needs and expectations from suppliers than would have been the case a few years ago.

- *Technological obsolescence is accelerating.* Product lifecycles are shortening. This trend has a positive advantage in that it keeps markets growing: these days we are unlikely to run into the old problem of Singer Sewing Machines who made products that would last for many years, but without introducing new technological advances that would make people want to upgrade to the next level. There is less time to exploit a new product or innovation than in the past. If too much time is spent on development, the product may be made obsolete by competitors' products before it is launched.

Plant and office equipment also become obsolete more quickly. The forerunner of the typewriter was invented in 1843. Some 30 years later Remington began production of a 'proper' typewriter. The mechanical typewriter became the office staple until after the Second World War, and still had a use in many offices up until the 1960s. Of course, there were improvements, but it was not uncommon to expect a 20- or 30-year life from a machine. Around the 1950s electric typewriters began to appear and became the norm in many offices by the 1960s. Innovations became more frequent, but again buyers could expect them to be long-lasting. Word processors using punched cards found their way into offices in the early 1970s, but were soon to become obsolete as computer technology was developed. Later in the

1970s electric typewriters gave way to electronic machines. The big acceleration in obsolescence came in the late 1970s and early 1980s when computer-based systems took over, expanding from typing to desktop publishing, and providing the ability to produce graphics and text as well as many other features. Innovation of software and hardware now means that few office computer systems have a useful life of more than about two or three years, leaving manufacturers of PCs with model lifecycles of between six and nine months. Certainly no one could contemplate going back to the long lifecycles of the precomputer age. Businesses that cannot afford to update, or that take too long in launching new innovations, have a great competitive disadvantage.

The pressure continues with the growth of the Internet, the change in methods of communication and the ever-expanding developments in the field of information handling.

- *Pressure to deliver shareholder value is increasing.* Top management of public companies has always had to balance the needs of shareholders for dividends and share price growth against the needs of the business. What became apparent throughout the 1980s was that many strategic actions taken by organizations reduced shareholder value. Porter (1987) drew attention to the ways in which the diversified organization could create value and pointed out that many did not do so. Recent research (KPMG, 2001) showed that organizations still have problems in addressing shareholder value. In its study of acquisitions in 2001, KPMG found that only 30% actually added shareholder value.

Among the many effects that shareholder pressure has had has been giving more focus to the issue of asset utilization. The 'make or buy' emphasis was mainly about cost reduction, but the shareholder value emphasis was one of the pressures that began to force more attention onto achieving higher profits while reducing the size of the asset investments needed to achieve those profits.

The large change in management metrics has been dramatic over the past 10 to 15 years, although somewhat ignored by academic researchers. These changes have led large firms, such as ICI, Unilever and IBM, to augment management's focus from volume in tonnage or units, revenue growth and margins, to include invested capital, asset utilization and leverage.

- *World recessions are periodic.* It used to be said that managers who had lived through the great depression that began with the 1929 Wall Street crash thereafter took a very different approach to their decision-making and were much more risk-averse. Like all generalizations it was probably only partly true. The careers of many of today's managers have included at least two world recessions and, in some cases, three. These too have had an effect on management behaviour, leading in many cases to shorter-term thinking and a belief in the formula of flat organizational structures and flexible organizations. Outsourcing has been seen as one way of aiding the achievement of the formula: sometimes it has been achieved without consideration of longer-term strategic issues and sometimes it has been undertaken with wisdom and common sense.

Influential concepts

Outsourcing is only one of the responses that organizations have made to external pressures. In addition to the other specific actions that have become commonplace, there have also been tools and methods influencing how managers think about outsourcing situations. However, not all organizations use all, or any, of the tools and methods, but even in those that use none, the thinking behind them will have had some impact.

Total Quality Management (TQM) is now well established in many organizations, and increased rapidly in popularity during the 1980s. TQM stresses the importance of collaboration between buyers and suppliers to replace what was commonly an antagonistic relationship. One dimension of this collaboration has been a reduction of the number of suppliers an organization deals with. Many organizations selected a smaller number of preferred suppliers from the larger number they had previously used. This different relationship between suppliers and buyers, with which many organizations now have some 10 to 20 years' experience, makes a shift to a different and even closer relationship – an incremental change in thinking rather than a quantum leap.

Core competencies have already been mentioned. Until the mid-1970s the conventional wisdom was that businesses should spread risk by diversifying into unrelated or loosely related fields. Few of these initiatives brought any synergy to the others and, as the spread of activities became wider, it became more difficult to provide all the capital needs of all the businesses. Many businesses failed to see opportunities for these initiatives, or failed to take advantage of those that they did see. From the early 1980s there was a new trend to divest many of these activities and use the funds generated to enhance the competitive positions of the strategic business units identified as core.

Prahalad and Hamel (1990) took this aspect of specialization a stage further, emphasizing the idea of concentrating not just on the core strategic business units but also on the core competencies that are essential for the business. Their approach was future-oriented in that the emphasis was on acquiring and maintaining the competencies needed today and also on using the concept dynamically to

Type of outsourcing	Examples	Buyer's decision drivers	Supplier's decision drivers
TRADITIONAL ACTIVITIES	Components Basic training course	Cost (make or buy analysis) TQM (single source)	Increased economies of scale Retaining customer
PERIPHERAL ACTIVITIES	Canteen operation Security services Cleaners Warehousing/delivery Tailored training course Subassemblies	Focusing management on higher priorities Improved performance levels Opportunities for reduced costs Avoiding hidden costs (e.g. labour turnover) Reducing problems from volume change	Increased/new business opportunities Medium-term customer tie-in Improve own performance
CRITICAL ACTIVITIES AND PROCESSES	Secure data backup Data processing Internal audit Recruitment Total facilities management	Increased value for money spent Management focus on strategic issues Higher levels of service Better use of scarce skills Reducing level of fixed assets	New business opportunities Longer-term customer tie in Learning curve effect Emphasis on core competencies
STRATEGIC AND PROBLEM-SOLVING ACTIVITIES	Corporate universities New product development R&D and sole source Total management of IT	Economies of scale in supply chain Focus on core competencies Higher quality delivered in these activities Reduction of fixed assets	Economies of scale Opportunity to capitalize on core competencies Potentially very long-term customer tie-in

Figure 1.1 – Hierarchy of outsourcing.

select the core competencies needed for future competitive success and to focus on these core competencies.

Figure 1.1 expresses the basic idea. Core competencies with a future orientation are central to this thinking. Other competencies appear in declining order of importance with the least valuable being those that are superfluous to present and future requirements. Although not all organizations have attempted to apply the core competencies concept, the underlying idea that there is a hierarchy of criticality has taken root and it is relevant when outsourcing is being considered.

The virtual organization is another old concept that emerged in a different guise in the early 1990s. Hedberg *et al.* (1994, p. 13) define the virtual organization using their preferred term 'the imaginary organization':

The perspective of the imaginary organization refers to a system in which assets, processes, and actors critical to the 'focal' enterprise exist and function both inside and outside the limits of the enterprise's conventional 'landscape' formed by its legal structure, its accounting, its organograms, and the language otherwise used to describe the enterprise.

In other words, it is possible to run a business and grow it to significant size without it owning the assets or employing the people who are used to produce the products and services it requires to function and ultimately to deliver value to the customers. The virtual company must possess core competencies that make individuals and other companies want to work with it. The lubricant of the virtual company is IT and fast, modern, communications that lessen the impact of distance. The virtual company may be achieved through a mix of arrangements, such as formal and informal alliances, subcontracting and buying in specialist services. Outsourcing may be used if it is changing from a conventional to a virtual company.

The term may be new, and more organizations may have followed the virtual route, but the underlying concept is old. Publishers, it could be argued, have been virtual companies for at least a hundred years. What they do *not* usually do in-house is:

- Write books
- Make a detailed review of books and proposals
- Design books
- Print books
- Copy edit and proofread
- Bind books
- Or, sometimes, market, sell and distribute books.

We think everyone would agree that, without the above, they would not be publishers! What are the particular competencies that enable them to function as publishers? These core competencies are the ability to attract authors to the firm, the commissioning of books that have a good prospect of selling, the shaping of their lists, the provision of financial resources to make the process work, the creation of an image for the imprint, and usually the marketing and selling. They are the main risk bearers. The whole is held together because it makes economic sense for all the other parties to work in this way.

The influence of the virtual organization concept goes beyond the number of organizations that will ever want to become virtual. It is reinforcement of the idea that a modern company does not have to do everything that it is currently doing, thus helping to open up thinking that challenges the status quo.

Supply chain management is another old concept that has been popularized in more recent years. The supply chain is the network of activities that begins with the primary raw materials and ends with the delivery of the product to the ultimate consumer. Numerous organizations participate in the supply chain and, because raw materials are supplied to and ubiquitous services are provided for various industries, many organizations are links in many supply chains.

Porter (1980) began to put the supplier back into strategic thinking with his Five Forces concept of industry analysis (suppliers, the industry, buyers, substitutes and entry/exit barriers). Five years later Porter extended his thinking with the development of the Value Chain concept. Porter argued that the firm provided value through a number of primary and support activities. These have to be disaggregated and analyzed in order to establish how the organization adds value and to identify the roots of its economic advantage. By controlling the key cost drivers, by finding ways to restructure the value chain and by optimizing the links between activities firms can gain advantage.

What can be done for a company within an industry can also be done for its suppliers and buyers, all with their own value chains. Supply chain management is about trying to optimize the linkages between the various firms so that value is improved for all the players. This concept provides an incentive to think positively about relationships with suppliers, and provides a conceptual platform on which to build outsourcing relationships in a way that puts both parties into a win situation.

Flexibility has been mentioned before. Because of the general turbulence of the environment, reinforced by the experiences of world recession, many organizations have reconfigured themselves so that they can reduce costs quickly. Much of this reconfiguration has taken place through flexible working practices. These practices may involve short-term contracts, greater use of part-time and agency employees, various flexible time arrangements with employees and outsourcing some activities. The aim is to enable the organization to adjust quickly to changes in volume without internal disruption and costs of redundancies.

Outsourcing today

The discussion so far has thrown up a series of more complex reasons for outsourcing than the original cost reduction argument of the 'make or buy' decision. Nonetheless, it still only scratches the surface of what is actually happening. Activities being outsourced have moved from the traditional areas to the strategic core of the organization, and are now even becoming an important part of the political agenda, both in Europe and the US. In the past it was sufficient to provide a simple list of the decision drivers, but it is now no longer sensible to treat all outsourcing decisions as identical. Similarly, different issues have to be faced by buyers and suppliers for each type of outsourcing and it is not sensible to ignore this.

We should state at the outset that Figure 1.1 shows a progression in complexity of outsourcing activities. We are not arguing that any stage in the figure is necessarily better than any other stage. It is also possible for an organization to have outsourcing arrangements under each of the classifications. The borders between each of our classification types are fuzzy, and some arrangements may have elements of more than one type. However, because it is difficult to perceive the precise borders does not invalidate the fact that there are differences. In an artist's palette we may not be able to precisely pinpoint when a pale blue turns to a pale green, but most of us can distinguish a bright green from a bright blue. We know that green is not the same as blue.

Traditional activities

The most basic form of outsourcing is the 'make or buy' type of decision. Typically it is a component that is outsourced, but it may be a service, such as the provision of a training course. The trigger may be a cost comparison, or it may be a change of some sort. For example, the company that made the 'Ovaltine' beverage in the UK was unusual in that until the early 1970s it made its own cans in an old can-making plant. 'Ovaltine' was in the decline stage of its lifecycle, and can-making was undergoing a number of changes in technology. To continue making cans would have meant that new investment would be required for what was already a small-scale production of cans at a time when volume was declining.

Cost comparisons can be tricky since they require an economic evaluation of all the factors that will change. These factors cannot be read directly from a cost accountant's statement of what a particular item costs to make. What is needed is an understanding of the costs that will remain with the organization when the component is outsourced, if these costs cannot be removed or redirected to a new economic activity. Superficial comparisons can lead to the wrong answer. It may be that a supplier can offer the component at x and the organization estimates that its total cost to make it is $2x$. However, if the $2x$ price includes labour costs that will not be removed or redirected to some other productive activity, and over-head costs like space and other allocations or apportionments that will remain whether or not the components are made, there may be no economic gain by outsourcing.

What drives the buyer's decision in this type of outsourcing situation? Usually it is to reduce current or anticipated costs. It may sometimes be related to a resource issue, such as freeing factory space for another activity, or a problem in obtaining scarce labour skills. There may be a TQM element. If some of the particular components were bought from a number of suppliers and others made in-house, consolidating them all with one preferred supplier may give opportunities for improved quality as well as reduced costs.

Of the supplier's decision drivers for outsourcing the first may be the opportunity to increase sales, although this decision may lead to other considerations, such as capacity increases. If the supplier is already supplying some of the particular component requirements, the opportunity to bid for the rest may be partly a defensive matter to retain the customer and to prevent a competitor from getting a foot in the door.

Typically we think of this sort of outsourcing decision in terms of normal buying and selling. However, the outsourcing effect may be obtained by a change in the buyer's materials management philosophy. Adopting a just-in-time (JIT) system may have the effect of outsourcing most of the inventory to suppliers. Dell is acknowl-edged as the world's most effective manufacturer of computers. It operates a JIT system and its factory in Eire holds the equivalent of four hours' inventory. It holds no stocks of components and some suppliers have built warehouses close to the plant so that they are better placed to meet the tight delivery schedules. No computers are built to be held in stock. Orders trigger production and the prod-uct is despatched as it reaches the end of the production line. JIT has been used for long enough for us to include it under the traditional classification, although it is very different from the 'make or buy' decision.

Peripheral activities

By this term we mean services that have to be undertaken but which, for the most part, require little industry-specific capability. A canteen is a canteen whether operated for an office or a factory, a computer manufacturer, or a steel works. Food and service requirements are relatively easy to specify. The organization might be inconvenienced if there was a total failure by the supplier but, because there are competitors in the marketplace, there could be a fast switch to a different supplier. Problems over quality can usually be addressed by discussion without a total breakdown of the service.

Security services and cleaning are other examples that have similar characteristics to canteen and company restaurant operations. The other three examples in Figure 1.1 have some different attributes as discussed below.

In the case of the warehousing and delivery outsourcing example, a failure has an impact on customers. In most situations, there is no reason to expect a service that is worse than that which the organization could provide itself. Getting the right level of service is a question of clarity in the contract. However, there are situations in which delivery within a promised period is so critical that very few suppliers can meet the requirements, in which case these warehousing and delivery activities would move into the 'critical activities and processes' category in Figure 1.1.

A highly tailored management training course differs from canteen operations in that it does require a knowledge of the organization, although this background may be learned by the supplier as part of the process of developing the course around the organization's problems. Such training courses are generally important, but many would not be critical in the sense that the organization would not suddenly collapse without them. A new supplier can be found within a reasonable period if the first one fails, and the overall aims of the training can still be met. However, again we can visualize situations in which the training may be vital for the success of an activity that is critical to the company, and it may even play a role in problem-solving. So, in some situations training could move into one of the remaining outsourcing categories because of the specific needs of the individual organization.

Subassemblies are right on the borderline. They are critical because, if they are not in place, the finished product cannot be produced. However, they may be no more critical than if all the components that go into them were outsourced. On balance, we feel that we have assessed their position accurately, again with the proviso that circumstances can alter cases.

The reasons behind the buyer's decision to outsource are likely to be more complex than for the traditional 'make or buy' decision. There may be opportunities to reduce costs to gain better performance, but many of these decisions will not reduce space costs and may not remove the need to supply other assets. A canteen or restaurant will use the same facilities as it did before it was outsourced. There is the advantage that existing employees who were performing this function can often be transferred to the supplier organization, thus avoiding severance costs and the loss of morale that redundancies might cause.

Perhaps the strongest decision driver is enabling management to focus on higher priorities. Of course, the supplier arrangement has to be administered and monitored, but otherwise there should be few problems. Any industrial relations issues among the outsourced staff would now be the responsibility of the supplier. Similarly, the buyer avoids the hidden costs of having to deal with the issues of labour turnover (temporary replacements, hiring and training new recruits). Overall, this arrangement may make it possible to reduce costs in areas such as human resources management, or to redirect the time saved on work of more long-term benefit to the organization.

There is also a shifting of future volume-change problems to the supplier. The extent to which this shift is possible depends on the nature of the contract between buyer and supplier, but in theory a specialist supplier with many customers can more easily adjust supply to demand because it has more opportunities to redeploy staff.

Suppliers have the chance to develop new business opportunities, sometimes involving a shift into different activities from, but related to, their current activities. They gain some security through the contracts under which they operate and higher volumes should bring opportunities for them to improve their own performance. Can they make money from these opportunities? That is the key question and, in general, the results show that they can.

Critical activities and processes

In this type of outsourcing arrangement the supplier is moving deeper into the core of the buyer's organization. All the activities are essential for the success of the buying organization and success means a close relationship between the two parties. If there is a failure, the consequences can be varying degrees of chaos. With this type of outsourcing the buyer's risk increases, which means that the decision drivers reflect a belief that the risks will be outweighed by the benefits to be gained.

There are degrees of criticality to outsourcing activities. The varying degrees of criticality are reflected in our view of the outsourcing hierarchy as a spectrum rather than a series of sharp steps. Examples of this type of outsourcing include several from the IT area, such as secure data backup and data processing. Failure in either can be serious, but data processing failures have the most immediate impact if things go wrong. At the far end of the spectrum is total facilities management. Facilities managed may be IT facilities, or may involve taking over the responsibility for staffing and managing a prison, hospital, or school in the public sector. Other examples of this type of outsourcing include internal audit and the total outsourcing of an entire human resources management activity such as recruitment or training.

What drives the buyer's decision? The answer is not the same in every case, but there are a number of common threads. For this type of decision the buyer may be seeking increased value for money spent, which may be a lower cost, but it is more likely to be increased reliability, a better product or service, or faster response times. As in the previous category, hassles are reduced and management time is freed up for concentrating on strategic issues. Particularly with the IT area, but elsewhere as well, outsourcing offers a way of solving skills shortages, not only for immediate vacancies but also for areas in which there is constant pressure because of technological advances and great external demand for persons with the requisite skills and expertise. For high-tech areas it may be a way of keeping the organization up to date as a specialist supplier is less likely to have pockets of long-serving employees in senior positions who are not quite keeping pace with new developments. In some situations, the supplier and not the buyer will own most of the assets, thereby freeing the buyer's resources for redeployment to other areas of the business.

Many new business activities have been created for suppliers. There is opportunity for longer-term customer tie-in: for example, the UK's Ministry of Defence signed a 12-year IT deal with EDS to provide payroll systems and services for the armed forces and pensioners (more about this example in the next chapter). The volumes of business that a specialist supplier can obtain are far greater than those of any one buyer, bringing a learning curve effect and economies of scale. The specialist suppliers are able to put emphasis on their own core competencies.

Strategic and problem-solving activities

Over time outsourcing arrangements have moved into our final classification, certainly covering many essential competencies (see Figure 1.1) and sometimes taking over what we should have considered to be core competencies, such as the food manufacturer with many of its strategic activities – the product research, market research, development and supply of flavourings – outsourced to a specialist organization. In terms of problem-solving activities, we look at activities leading to the provision of a total solution, which we define as *an integrated offering of know-how, services and/or products sold to a customer on specific terms and conditions including criteria of satisfaction.*

The special aspect of solutions is that they are a combination of services and products – that is, intangible and tangible goods. For the seller, the challenge is to be able to define and understand the customer's criteria of satisfaction – which are not always based on technical or hard standards – and make them operational.

Total solutions may be combined with facilities management. We see facilities management as *total solutions that also involve ongoing management responsibilities necessitating integrated co-ordination with the client organization.*

The special aspect concerning facilities management is the management responsibility, specifically the managerial responsibility that the seller has over employees at the buyer's premises. Therefore, when undertaking facilities management contracts, companies must not only deliver a product and/or service on specific terms and conditions including criteria of satisfaction, but also have managerial responsibility for employees at the client's premises. Often these are former employees of the client.

Examples of activities of this type of outsourcing include 'corporate universities' in which almost all activities are delegated to a supplier, usually a university, and the total management of the whole of the IT operations. Design management, new product development and research and development in specific areas are highly strategic and problem-solving activities for which the buyer requires a total solution.

Buyers take this type of decision in order to focus more closely on what they see as the core competencies of the organization. They may be not so much shedding expense as shedding the responsibility for retaining high levels of expertise in areas that are technologically advanced or changing rapidly, areas for which the future costs of staying in the forefront are thought to be very high. This sort of arrangement sets out to maximize the benefits that can be extracted from the supply chain and has the potential to create a win–win situation for both parties. As with our previous category such an arrangement may bring a reduction of assets, thereby improving ROI, even if total costs are unchanged.

Many suppliers are moving into uncharted waters when they take on this type of activity. Although a number may have been in their industry for many years, this type of relationship is new. Despite the fact that new competencies have to be mastered, the business opportunity may bring economies of scale and the opportunity to gain greater rewards from their own core competencies as well as providing the volume of activity that makes it economic for them to hone these competencies and develop new value-adding services. Potentially they have the opportunity to develop very long-term relationships with their clients, with these relationships becoming more like alliances than normal purchasing/supplying activities.

In the next chapter we will look more about the issues buyers and suppliers have to face as they enter into the various types of outsourcing relationships.

Summary

In this chapter we have looked at the historical roots of outsourcing–insourcing and the current trends. There is a clear trend over time showing that outsourced activities are moving from the traditional areas to the strategic core of the organization. We have discussed our classification of the types of outsourcing activities and examples of each as well as the decision drivers for buyers and sellers. We begin to address the central question: *Can money be made from the new relationship opportunities?* by starting to show where money-making opportunities lie.

References

Anthony, R. A. and Reece, J. S. 1978. *Accounting text and cases*, 6th edition, Irwin, Homewood, IL.

Hamel, G. and Prahalad, P. K. 1994. *Competing for the future*, Harvard Business Review Press, Boston, MA.

Hedberg, B., Dahlgren, G., Hansson, J. and Olve, N.-G. 1994. *Virtual organizations and beyond*, John Wiley & Sons, Ltd, Chichester.

KPMG 2001. *World class transactions: Insights into creating shareholder value*, KPMG, London.

Nohria, N. (ed.) 1998. *The portable MBA desk reference*, 2nd edition, John Wiley & Sons Inc, New York.

Pearce, D. W. (ed.) 1983. *The dictionary of modern economics*, Revised edition, Macmillan, London.

Porter, M. E. 1980. *Competitive strategy*, Free Press, New York.

Porter, M. E. 1985. *Competitive advantage*, Free Press, New York.

Porter, M. E. 1987. From competitve advantage to corporate strategy, *Harvard Business Review*, May–June.

Prahalad, P. K. and Hamel, G. 1990. The core competence of the corporation, *Harvard Business Review*, May–June.

Semlinger, C. 1991. New developments in subcontracting: Mixing market and hierarchy, in Amin, A. and Dietrich, M. (eds), *Towards a New Europe? - structural change in the European economy*, Edward Elgar, Aldershot.

2 Moving to supplying total solutions

Introduction

In the previous chapter we considered a hierarchy of outsourcing situations. Although there is no inevitability about progressing through each of the various stages, the reality is that many organizations do. In this chapter we consider the process by which a firm moves to supplying total solutions. We also consider the management implications of the four different types of outsourcing activities that were presented in Chapter 1. Two case studies are presented.

Management issues for outsourced activities

For each of the types of outsourcing activities identified in Chapter 1 (Figure 1.1) there are management issues – management issues for buyers of the solutions and management issues for the sellers of the solutions. There is no merit to the argument that buying organizations must strive to reach the strategic and problem-solving level of outsourcing activities, the most complex form of outsourcing activities – the risks and benefits are, to some degree, dependent on the organization itself. However, it is important to draw attention to the differences between the traditional activity level and the various stages thereafter. Those firms that do progress to the second level will have built experience and knowledge of outsourcing that may help to develop the confidence to try out the third level. Whether

Type of outsourcing	Examples	Buyer's management issues	Supplier's management issues
TRADITIONAL ACTIVITIES	Components Basic training course	Collaborative purchasing Relatively low risk Can change supplier	Customer service management How to maintain privileged role
PERIPHERAL ACTIVITIES	Canteen operation Security services Cleaners Warehousing/delivery Tailored training course Subassemblies	Adequate administrative control Issues when own employees taken over Ensure standards clear from outset Ability to break the link with notice Risks low	Responsible managing Monitor own performance Regular discussion with client Culture of service at all levels How many customers for security?
CRITICAL ACTIVITIES AND PROCESSES	Secure data backup Data processing Internal audit Recruitment Total facilities management	Management and admin control Multi-level supplier contact Handling internal HR issues Risks high if supplier fails Some internal culture change Build relationship	Risks high if client damaged Size of contracts may be large Mirror client contact needs Strong customer service culture Understand client's business Relationships with many clients
STRATEGIC AND PROBLEM-SOLVING ACTIVITIES	Corporate universities New product development R&D and sole source Total management of IT	Risks very high if supplier fails Numerous multi-level relationships Strong collaborative/alliance culture Relationships longer term	Mirror client contact needs Exceed performance levels Flexible to cope with many clients Collaborative/alliance culture

Figure 2.1 – Examples of management issues.

an organization makes a slow progression into the deeper waters, or dives in head first to brave the more difficult and complex depths, there should be no assumption that the management issues are the same for each stage. This statement applies to suppliers as well as buyers.

Figure 2.1 is really an extension of Figure 1.1, and the first two columns of both are the same. Where the figures differ is in the addition of certain management issues to supplement the decision drivers explored in Figure 1.1. The issues, with some variation in circumstances, refer to all the examples and other similar outsourcing situations.

Traditional activities

The traditional type of outsourcing activity needs little discussion, except to mention that a critical task for the supplier is to maintain the relationship. Maintaining relationships may mean thinking more widely about the needs of the customer and developing a customer-friendly culture at all levels having contact with the buyer. The seeds of a collaborative relationship can be sown in this type of relationship. Through collaborative relationships both parties may move to a more complex type of outsourcing relationship. Suppliers have to ensure that their prices are still competitive, a task that involves a process of continuous improvement coupled with awareness of competitive rates. Buyers have to accept, if relationships are to be successful, that suppliers have to make reasonable profits.

Peripheral activities

For many of the peripheral activities there is a major difference between the supplier and the buyer. Buyers may outsource each particular service to individual suppliers. There may be some exceptions as a result of location or policy: for example, different suppliers in various parts of the country may provide security or cleaning services.

Most suppliers, however, will serve a number of buyers. Suppliers generally provide services to many organizations, and indeed this is the only way for them to manage the impact of loss of a contract: any total business set up to service only one customer will always walk on the knife edge. Success for the buyer with this type of outsourcing is more a matter of administrative skills than of management.

As we saw in Chapter 1, the risk to the buyer is relatively low for most of these activities because in theory the cost of switching suppliers is not high and there is a competitive market. However, switching depends on the care with which contracts are prepared, both in terms of provisions for termination and articulation of performance standards. It can be costly for a buyer to unilaterally terminate a live contract, particularly if expectations and standards of performance are so ill-defined that it becomes difficult to find legal grounds for termination.

Measurement of satisfaction with the supplier on an ongoing basis is more a matter of establishing measurement systems, discussing issues with the supplier as they arise, and only alerting higher levels of management when there appears to be a very serious problem emerging. Contemporaneous records, such as details of each occasion on which the cleaning supplier has to be called in because parts of the building have not been properly cleaned, are particularly important when performance data cannot be obtained from a routine information system. Good record keeping is essential for the buying organization to ensure that it is getting what was expected from the outsourcing contract and it could provide vital evidence in a serious contractual dispute.

Once the switch to outsourcing has been made, the changes in structure in the buying organization are nominal. The changes are concerned mainly with ensuring that there are clear lines of responsibility for the management and administration of each supplier. There is little effect on the optimum culture of the organization since each activity outsourced is off to one side of the main activities and services usually continue in much the same way as before.

The initial issue that the buying organization has to tackle is what to do with the employees who are working in the area to be outsourced. Outsourcing may result in a redundancy situation, but it is more likely that these employees will be taken over by the supplier to whom the contract is awarded. However, takeover of the employees does not necessarily remove all the issues that may emerge, or mean that the organization can take decisions without employee consultation. Many hospitals in the British National Health Service have outsourced peripheral services such as cleaning and the employees have been transferred to the private supplying company. However, there is considerable hostility from trade unions because, although the terms and conditions of transferred employees are protected, suppliers are not bound to offer the same conditions to future new employees.

A large number of supplier organizations have been set up to service the cleaning and facilities management sector of the outsourcing market, some of which have several decades of experience. Taking over an organization's employees is not a problem for an expanding business, nor is it for those businesses that have a high labour turnover. A large specialist organization serving many buyers will have opportunities to move employees to other local contracts, and potentially can offer greater development opportunities for some types of employee than would have been the case with their former employer.

Important contributors to success include skills that enable the supplying company to understand the client's needs as they evolve and to meet these needs. Regular management interface with the buying organization is essential to ensure that problems are solved early and in a way that satisfies the client.

Critical activities and processes

Both the buyer and the supplier face higher risks as outsourcing activity moves into critical activities and for both parties there are many more strategic and organizational issues to consider if outsourcing is to succeed for both parties. A culture that creates a partnership between the two organizations has to be present to a far greater extent than for traditional activities or peripheral activities.

This type of outsourcing is increasing in the private sector and the public sector. In the public sector in the UK outsourcing activities often go under various names, including public finance initiative (PFI) and public private partnerships (PPP), and the initiatives have been far-reaching. As a result, there are useful lessons that can be learned from both sectors, but there is the additional advantage that in the UK the National Audit Office (1999) conducts detailed enquiries into the success of such initiatives. It is useful to look at the issues that have arisen from one such outsourcing situation.

Case study: The 1999 crisis at the UK Passport Agency

The Passport Agency handled all the tasks for the issue of new passports. It was realized that the existing computer system could not cope with the expected demand for passports and, in any case, the equipment was near the end of its useful life. A business plan was prepared to evaluate the various options, a result of which was a decision to outsource two of the three major components of the passport system. In addition to the intention to replace old equipment, there was also the intention to change to a digital passport because it was believed that this step would reduce forgeries.

One key reason for outsourcing, in addition to expected lower processing costs, was the transfer of risks to the private sector. The Agency expected that its contractors would take responsibility for 'system design and implementation, maintaining service levels, responding to changes in the volume of applications, and providing technological updates and project financing' (National Audit Office, 1999).

The outsourcing contracts

The decision to outsource two of the three functions at the Passport Agency was taken in July 1996. The agency retained the examination and authorization function, which had the key tasks of checking data accuracy, assessing eligibility for passports, authorizing their issue, answering telephone and postal queries and maintaining counter service.

In June 1997 the contact was awarded to Siemens Business Services for the outsourcing of the initial processing function. The key tasks were to open postal applications, log their receipt, check and bank fees, check that forms were completed correctly and had the appropriate enclosures, refer queries to applicants, scan applications into the system and check the accuracy of data scanning. In addition, Siemens was contracted to provide a new computer system to support application processing and printing interface.

Three other firms were short listed along with Siemens, with final negotiations being conducted with Siemens and EDS. The contract awarded to Siemens was for 10 years and had an estimated value of £120 million, although much of this fee was to be paid on a per-passport-processed basis. It was estimated that 400 Agency staff would transfer to Siemens.

The Stationery Office (since renamed Security Printing and Systems Ltd) was awarded the contract for the secure printing and despatch of passports in July 1997. In order to meet the need for urgent passports it had to provide and maintain equipment in the various passport offices and to print and despatch the majority of passports from a central location. This contract also was for 10 years with an estimated cost of £120 million.

Rolling out the new system

The intention was that the new system and outsourcing arrangements would be rolled out to the regional offices over the period between October 1998 and February 1999 beginning with the largest office Liverpool (26% of volume), followed by Newport (24%) and Peterborough (24%). The roll-out process began on schedule in Liverpool, at which time 100 employees transferred to Siemens. The expectation was that output would reach 30 000 issues a week in Liverpool by mid-November. In reality, it had hit only 8000 issues by this time. Nevertheless, the Passport Agency decided to continue the roll-out to Newport with a further 96 people transferring to Siemens. In Newport, as in Liverpool, the output targets were not met. In late November the Passport Agency agreed with its partners that the roll-out should be halted until the problems had been resolved in the first two locations.

The Liverpool problem was partly caused by errors in the scanning process resulting in a higher-than-expected number of corrections by the operators. There had also been some changes to the design of the system to give increased security. Knock-on effects included a lowering of productivity by the examiners because of unfamiliarity of the system and insufficient support to help with queries about the new system. A separate problem related to the urgent passports, which Siemens could not always scan as quickly as the Agency wanted, in part because the new on-site printers provided by the other outsourcing contractor did not always work as well as expected.

The decision to roll out at Newport was taken with many reservations. One factor was that the accommodation at Newport had already been reconfigured and recabled and staff had been trained; as a result, it would not be easy to revert to the old system. There was considerable justification for this view because the postponement of the Peterborough roll-out caused similar problems and the loss of 10 days' output. Equally important was the fact that, without the Newport roll-out, it would not be possible to reach the minimum annual volume of the new digital passports that had been guaranteed to the other outsourcing partner and, as a consequence, compensation of up to £3 million would have to be paid by the Agency.

1999

The Agency entered 1999 with a much-reduced capacity because of the problems at the Liverpool and Newport sites, despite switching work from those centres to other offices and also increasing staffing levels and overtime work. The capacity problems brought a steady increase in the backlog of unprocessed passports, exacerbated by an increase in demand that was greater than had been forecast: it was the first year that babies had to have their own passports. As delays increased, so did the level of enquiries about late passports and demand increased still more as the public, realizing that it took longer to obtain a new passport, began to send applications in earlier.

At the peak of the problem in June 1999 there was a backlog of 565 000 unprocessed passports, representing over a month's work. Photographs appeared in the national press of queues outside the London passport office as an increasing number of would-be travellers became concerned about getting their passports in time. The final costs of the delays included the purchase of umbrellas to hand to those forced to queue for hours in the rain and the provision of luncheon vouchers for them.

Emergency measures included allowing passports to be extended for two years, free of charge, at Post Offices. These measures, plus the seasonal slowing of demand, meant that processing times could be reduced to the 10-day target by the end of August 1999.

The costs of it all

The failure of the outsourcing to deliver according to the plan had cost implications for both the Passport Agency and its outsourcing partners.

The National Audit Office report estimated the costs of the failure to the public purse as nearly £12.6 million. Included in this figure was compensation to the printing partner of £680 000 because the volume of digital passports was lower than the minimum guaranteed figure and £110 000 to members of the public who incurred losses because they could not travel. Six million pounds were spent on additional staff and overtime costs, nearly £3 million on payments to the Post Office for free extensions and nearly £2 million on running both the new and the old systems because of the problems with the roll-out. The overall amount also includes a figure of £69 000 for service credits received from the two outsourcing partners.

The National Audit Office quoted the Agency's estimated unit cost of producing a passport at between £15.00 and £15.50, compared to the target of £12 and, although the long-term effect was not known at the time of the NAO report at the end of October 1999, the future cost was estimated to be £14. Part of the increase was for the additional security enhancements requested by the Agency, which had an effect on supplier costs and the amount of equipment required. The unit charge per passport paid to Siemens increased by 14% from the contract value of £2.39, and Security Printing received a 10% increase on its contract charge per passport of £2.92.

The crisis was also expensive for the outsourcing partners, particularly Siemens. This company had paid £65 000 of the service credits mentioned above, and owed an estimated £60 000 more. In theory, Siemens should have paid a further £275 000 between the start of the roll-out to the end of June 1999. The service charges had been waived over this period, in part because the scanning problem was caused by the application forms, for which the design had to be changed at the Agency's request, and in part because of a heavier demand than that forecast by the Agency. Under the contract Siemens was required to process routine applications and make them available for examination within 15 hours of receipt by post, and there were penalties if the target was not met. In reality, the amount waived should have been higher, perhaps by £120 000 because the recording system began when letters were opened, whereas it should have started when letters were received. This error was rectified starting in July 1999.

Service payments of this sort were only the smaller part of the costs Siemens incurred. The company had to bear the costs of recruiting and employing an extra 60 staff at Liverpool and Newport, on top of its original complement of 155. The decision to postpone the roll-out reduced Siemens' income for 1999–2000 from the expected £14 million to only £5.4 million. In addition, the crisis would have increased the management costs of the contract.

From the NAO's figures, it appears that contractual compensation to Security Printing was far greater than the small amount of service payments to the Agency of £4000. However, this organization also had many hidden costs because of the crisis and the changes in plan.

The Passport Agency example makes the point that outsourcing critical activities and processes can create dangers for both buyers and suppliers. It is possible to criticize the agency (and Siemens) for moving too quickly and, in hindsight, it could have been less catastrophic to have begun with the smallest office and allowed a longer period for dealing with the teething problems before rolling out to the next phase.

It is likely that many of the problems of the new system would have occurred even if there had been no outsourcing at the same time. In this situation, the difficulties were compounded because the digital imaging, which was the core of the system, meant a complete change of working methods throughout the Agency. At the far end of the process, the method for producing passports had also changed with a reliance on the integration of the computer system with the printing methods. Because two outsourcing partners were brought in, there were three organizations required to work closely together, necessitating interfaces at various levels and at various locations.

Although the buying organization still retains the core competencies in this type of outsourcing decision, it has to place great reliance on its outsourcing partners. The Passport Agency experience shows the seriousness of the problems that can arise if things do not go smoothly. If there are problems, the buying organization may incur loss of revenue, extra costs and loss of customer confidence, all of which can have a long-term effect. The core competencies may be what the future of the organization will be built on, but a failure of other critical activities can mean that it never reaches that future.

So the outsourcing of critical activities and processes is not a decision to be taken lightly. It requires careful financial evaluation, which should include risk analysis. From this analysis should come decisions about what the buying organization wants to see written into the commercial contract. However, carefully written contracts are not enough to ensure a smooth transition to outsourcing. Both parties to the contract need to examine their own operations to see how they can ensure an effective working relationship.

Issues of interface of personnel at various levels must be worked out and mechanisms established for the early identification and resolution of problems and difficulties. This step is particularly important for certain situations (for example, the design problems with the forms used for passport applications in the UK Passport Agency case) in which the actions of one of the parties have an effect on the performance of the other. Perhaps one of the biggest cultural changes that may be needed in some organizations is a greater emphasis on consultation with shared decision-making for certain types of decisions. Training is important. The National Audit report on the Passport Agency found that the computer system was defined and its operating procedures made available in time for Siemens to train its own staff. Unfortunately, the supporting clerical procedures were not available at the time the Agency trainers (who had also been trained by Siemens) had to train the Agency staff. A good training programme should do more than raise the level of competence of the employees directly involved; it should provide an understanding of the overall concept to the organization as a whole in addition to helping individuals to become comfortable with their own particular roles. Control systems must be put in place so that both parties have the information needed to monitor performance and to be satisfied that any penalty clauses in the contract are fairly administered. Fairness is more difficult to achieve than to suggest. In the Passport Agency example, the performance of Siemens was affected by the following factors:

- Increases in demand for passports above the assumptions on which the Agency had founded its business case
- Changes to the system design introduced at the request of the Agency
- Deficiencies in the application form
- Low initial productivity because of other factors, such as delays in information, or complexity in interactions with Agency staff.

The output problem was only partly attributable to Siemens, but reaching agreement on the size of that part was a complex issue.

The supplying partner faces particular risks of a different kind. First, there are what might be termed the project risks, which are increased because the supplier usually has to build its bid for the business on figures supplied by the buyer. Siemens, for example, is unlikely to have had any capability to query the forecasts of passport volumes, although performance is to a degree dependent on the figures. When the supplier is responsible for both the capital and the revenue expenditures and when much of the equipment is dedicated to the contract and kept on buyer premises, there is a vulnerability to volume changes.

There are also commercial risks associated with the standing of the buying organization. WorldCom provides an example upon which we can reflect with the benefit of hindsight.

Responding in 2002 to questions related to the WorldCom debacle,[1] EDS stated that it would continue to supply IT-outsourcing services to the telecoms giant under an 11-year $6.4 billion contract signed in October 1999 and that payments were up to date.

In the longer term, however, EDS admitted that developments at WorldCom could affect its operational results in 2002, but said that it would not be 'material' to its financial position.

Under existing IT services agreements WorldCom was expected to contribute revenue of $160–175 million and earnings per share of 3–4 cents in each of the last two quarters of 2002.

The collapse of WorldCom following its crisis of misrepresentation of its profits left many partners unhappy. Not every outsourcing partner has partners as large as WorldCom, but many would suffer severe economic shocks if a major partner were to go under.

A third area of risk is the knock-on effect if a client's reputation is damaged by the outsourcing activity. To a large degree, the supplier's reputation becomes entwined with that of the buyer. A British example is the outsourcing of railway maintenance and safety inspection.

Railtrack PLC took ownership of the track, signals, stations, etc., and outsourced the routine maintenance and safety inspections and work to a series of other companies, each responsible for a defined geographical area. A number of high-profile rail crashes and breaches

---

[1] *Management Consultants' News Direct*, Issue 40, 8 July 2002.

of safety led to the government putting Railtrack into administration and the phoenix that rose from the ashes is a not-for-profit company, Network Rail. Although there is no evidence that the outsourcing arrangements are less effective than the in-house system run by British Rail before the railways were privatized, the issue has attracted considerable media attention. There is evidence of faulty maintenance and accusations of forged record keeping by employees of some of the outsourcing partners. It has also been argued that inadequate training is being given to new recruits in the maintenance companies and that, in any case, many recruits are agency personnel and not employees of those companies. Some of the accusations are made by trade union personnel with a political agenda – the renationalization of the railways – and have to be interpreted in this light. However, there can be no doubt that the image of Railtrack and its outsourcing suppliers has been tarnished to an extent that may do long-term damage to some of them.

It is, of course, the scale of the business opportunity that is attractive to suppliers, and much of it may be new business that builds on the foundations of the historic business. But it is only good business if both parties are satisfied with the result. So the supplier, too, needs to evaluate each opportunity very carefully, including an assessment of the risks.

It may be that after this risk assessment the supplier feels a need to negotiate the terms of the contract, rather than just responding to the terms that the buyer specifies. It is interesting that the National Audit report on the Passport Agency mentions that there were other organizations short listed for both the outsourcing contracts, but that only the two winners put in bids that were fully compliant with the required contract terms. For both contracts, the issues that other suppliers could not accept concerned future price reductions and the various penalties and indemnities. Obviously, it is sound advice for a supplier to walk away from a bid involving conditions that it deems unwise to accept.

The costs of the larger bids can be very high. For example, it has been reported that two of the organizations that have a large stake in this type of outsourcing, Jarvis and Amey, were spending £1 million per month each preparing for the long-awaited PPI initiative for the London Underground. In most cases, there can be only one winner, but several losers, all of whom have incurred very high up-front expenditures to prepare bids. As it may take a considerable time before contracts are awarded, there can be serious cash flow consequences for both the winner and the loser. A recent change in accounting practice means that bid costs in the UK have to be expensed when incurred, instead of being capitalized and written off over time. This requirement provides another reason for great care by a supplier in deciding whether to bid for a particular contract. Interestingly, one of the major UK players in this type of outsourcing, Amey, was in 2002 reported to be giving up bidding for government PFI and PPP work, despite the fact that the volume of this work is planned to increase significantly. Amey is currently involved in public and private sector outsourcing in rail, roads, health, schools and defence.

Suppliers have to work hard to make outsourcing contracts work. Because they cover critical areas, they are high profile within the buying organization, and because not every employee of that organization will be enthusiastic about outsourcing, there may be many who will seek ways to find fault. The best defence is to make sure that there are no grounds for complaint.

The necessary steps include:

- Ensuring that the employees of the supplying partner understand the buyer's organization and its business. This step has to involve an in-depth understanding that is at least as good as would have been the case had the employees been on the buyer's payroll.
- Setting up an appropriate structure for each contract to, take account of the interface with the buyer as well as with the rest

of the supplier organization. The issue is complicated by the fact that initially there may be two very different management teams required, possibly overlapping: the Passport Agency example showed that Siemens had a project management issue to deal with before this issue was overlapped by an operational management problem.

- Clarifying the expectations of both parties. For example, how far is the supplier expected to interface with various parts of the buyer organization in which it may not currently be working so that technology changes can be factored into issues such as the buyer's new product development?
- Establishing information systems that allow all aspects of the contract to be monitored and that enable problems to be identified early, and preferably avoided.
- Developing an open culture with the buyer to facilitate better communication.

From the supplying organization's viewpoint there is an added complication in that it may have similar contracts with a variety of organizations, each with different organizational and cultural requirements, even if the technologies are similar. This matter brings a substantial challenge to suppliers when they are deciding how to structure their activities.

Strategic and problem-solving activities

The conventional wisdom about outsourcing has been that the organization should retain the core competencies in-house, and only consider outsourcing those activities that are non-core. As we have already seen, this concept can be pushed to the limit when critical activities and processes are outsourced and there are a growing number of situations in which outsourcing has been taken a step further and moved into the strategic core of the organization.

We mentioned in the previous chapter that there is some blurring at the edges between this particular type of outsourcing and the previous type, partly because what is core is largely a subjective decision taken in the context of the particular organization and the vision it holds of its future. Therefore, it is quite possible for two apparently identical organizations to take a totally different view of what is core, or for a change in top management to trigger a totally different outlook. In fact, there are many practical examples of the impact of senior management changes. We have only to think of the changes at Pearson, the international media company that produces textbooks and other products such as the *Financial Times* and Penguin Books, over the past few years. During this period various newly acquired businesses were sold off following the arrival of a chief executive with a different vision for the group. Marconi, the telecommunications equipment company, provides a more dramatic example. The new chief executive divested the company of many of its long-standing businesses in order to invest in telecommunications with the result that the company was almost destroyed. If such wide variations can exist in what is seen as core businesses, how much wider the scope is for different viewpoints about what are the core competencies within those businesses!

Case study: The European Chewing Gum Company (identity disguised)

The company had been founded in 1915 and began to make chewing gum in 1927. By 2000 it had an annual turnover of around €200 million, a figure that had been roughly static for the previous five years. By this time the company had evolved into an international player, focusing on the development, production, marketing and sales of international brands. It operated in most of Europe and also had networking and cooperative alliances with companies such as Kraft, Suchard, Freis Marabou and Smith-KlineBeecham.

The provision of flavours is a core competence in chewing gum production and flavours are often the basis for the development of new products. Although the industry generally did not manufacture its own flavours, European Chewing Gum undertook its own research and development as well as market research, as did its competitors. During the late 1990s the company began a key supplier programme. The aims were to reduce the time spent on routine supply decisions and to obtain more knowledge from suppliers, specifically through working with suppliers who could quickly adjust to changes in customer preferences. The criteria for selecting the key supplier of flavours included the obvious issues of quality, hygiene and R&D capability. However, other factors such as the capability and willingness of the supplier to collaborate, willingness to share knowledge and understanding of the market were very important.

Once the key supplier had been selected and the relationship was working, it was a relatively small step to outsource other aspects of flavours to that supplier. European Chewing Gum now relies completely on its outsourcing partner for all the market research and R&D on flavours. Its own R&D department is now part of the marketing department and it concentrates on product development.

The chewing gum case study is an example of what is occurring. It is still only a minority of organizations that progress to this step, but what is a minority activity today may become the norm tomorrow. The ultimate in transition in outsourcing, the virtual organization, is beyond the scope of our figure on outsourcing activities. In a virtual organization almost all activities are outsourced in one way or another. It is unlikely that a majority of organizations will ever take this step, if only because it is simply not possible to end up with a totally virtual economy. Somewhere along the supply chain there have to be some organizations that actually own and deploy assets.

In the next chapter we will look at the implications of supplying total solutions for marketing and sales force management.

Summary

The transition to supplying total solutions has been discussed in terms of a detailed example of outsourcing at the UK Passport Agency. The transition to the two modern forms of outsourcing – critical activities and processes and also strategic and problem-solving activities – is to creating some very large supplier businesses. Certain of the bids, particularly in IT, are too complex for an individual supplier and it is common for consortia involving, for example, a management consulting firm, a systems provider and a computer manufacturer, to be formed. The potentially substantial revenues arising from the two modern types of outsourcing are accompanied by costs and risks and they bring issues that are more familiar to contracting businesses than to many traditional supplier businesses. It is not only the buyer who has to beware.

Reference

National Audit Office 1999. *The passport delays of summer 1999*, NAO, London.

3 Retooling marketing and the sales force

Find the right prospect, at the right time, and close the deal.
Brochure of Impact Sales Inc. (sales force for hire company)

Introduction

As the increase in outsourcing continues, companies are finding that their marketing and sales efforts also must be re-evaluated. In this chapter, we explore some of the ways in which the changes to the marketplace are affecting marketing and sales force management. The traditional approaches used by companies for marketing and for managing their sales force personnel must be re-examined on the basis of the new buyer/seller relationships that characterize the provision of total solutions in outsourcing. We discuss some strategies that companies can use for marketing and sales force management in connection with their efforts to capture outsourcing business contracts in general and provision of total solutions in particular.

The search for a better way to trap mice

As firms become enchanted with the opportunities in outsourcing they find that merely wishing to sell 'value added' rarely provides successful outcomes. Most managers and marketing savants know that few decisions a firm makes are more critical than its selection of the market to be served. This is clearly also the case in the markets for outsourced solutions and complex projects. Customers' functional and relationship requirements dictate the required solution characteristics. Purchasing policies and customer values dictate the nature of buyer/seller relations and the communication effort. Levels of competition and customer sensitivity to price significantly influence pricing policies. Size of targeted customers and their preferences can influence, and sometimes determine, choice of delivery mechanisms and mode of interaction.

In broad terms a *market* can be defined as *those potential customers who share a similar want or need and who are able and willing to commit their funds and resources to satisfy that want or need* (Hayes *et al.*, 1996). However, similar wants and needs may be subject to much variation. Having elected to participate in a given market, it is then necessary to decide what segment(s) of the market can feasibly be served with a given marketing strategy or mix, and to what extent the marketing strategy needs to be varied in order to accommodate variation in the customers' wants and needs. We define a *market segment* as *a group of potential customers who are likely to respond similarly to one or more elements of a marketing strategy*. Thus, *market segmentation* is *the process of identifying those segments that can feasibly be targeted and that represent profitable opportunities for the firm*. In some instances, firms can achieve their aspirations for growth or financial performance by focusing on just one segment. In other instances, achievement of goals may require targeting several segments. To target multiple segments may require variation in just one element of the marketing strategy, such as the promotional message, or it may require variation in all the strategy elements of the bundle of goods, services, delivery mechanisms, relationship mechanisms and pricing/risks schemes.

Competitive forces and unique customer requirements suggest the merits of defining segments narrowly. Economies of scale and scope, with respect to marketing as well as operations, argue for a broader definition of a segment, or aggregation of several segments. Therefore, the final match of marketing strategy to a segment, or segments, will depend on the particular situation of the firm.

For some firms, their outsourcing strategy will dictate a very narrow segment definition containing only few firms, as for instance has been the case with some of the first-tier producers in the automotive sector. For most firms, the issue is more complex. Should it target several segments of potential customers or just a particular subset? Would one marketing plan be suitable for all customers? If not, should a number of plans be developed, each tailored for a particular set of homogeneous customers, or should the company develop just one plan focused on a single homogeneous segment? And furthermore, what characteristics would indicate homogeneity? Would the size of the firm or the nature of its product be sufficient indicators of homogeneity, or would it be necessary to take other variables into account?

Consider the case of Semco, a Danish service company that has evolved its services over many years, as depicted in Figure 3.1.

This evolution has meant that Semco's original customer base has also had to evolve, as have the competitors it is meeting in the marketplace. The firm acknowledges that this development has

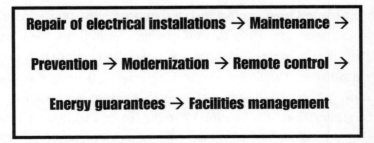

Figure 3.1 – Evolution of Semco's 'bundle of goods and services.

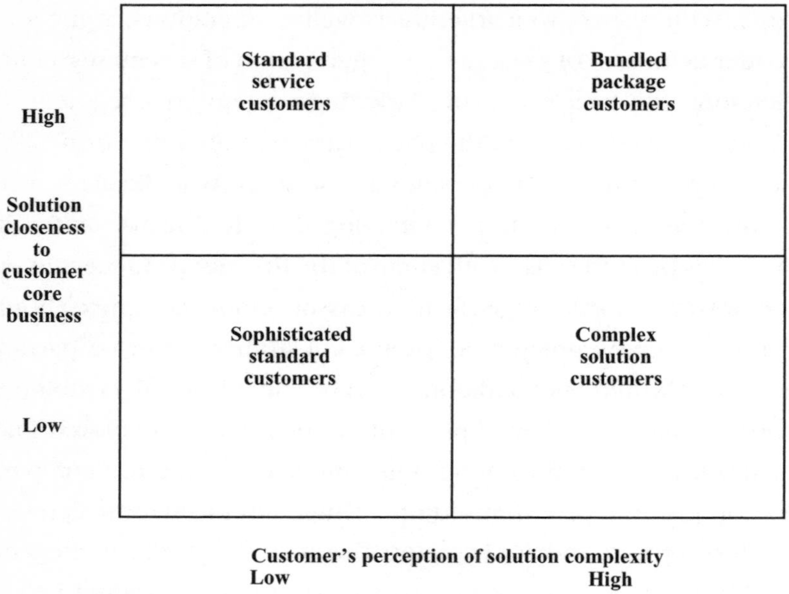

High	Standard service customers	Bundled package customers
Solution closeness to customer core business		
Low	Sophisticated standard customers	Complex solution customers

Customer's perception of solution complexity
Low   High

Figure 3.2 – Semco's segmentation framework.

partly been driven by its effort to protect its core base, and notes that the evolution of its customer base has stimulated its need to build new competencies. The company has used a simple framework to segment its current and potential customer base as shown in Figure 3.2 above.

It is intuitively attractive to contemplate the following scenario: finding a market segment that responds more favourably to the firm's marketing strategies than to those of its competitors for a product that closely meets its wants and needs and one that is potentially profitable. The search for such segments, however, is highly situation-specific. With new-to-the-world offerings, for instance, precise segmentation may be difficult and market selection may need to be broad, taking into account a wide range of possibilities. When Giantcode, a European development company for new materials technologies, introduced novel solutions for making moulding tools, it had to focus on a broad range of potential customers. By contrast, in mature industries the search for new segments may focus on narrow segments, requiring modification to only a small part of the marketing strategy.

Examples abound of firms that successfully serve a particular segment – so successfully, in some cases, that they dominate the segment to the exclusion of competitors. A number of approaches have been developed to materially assist with the search for characteristics that might identify customers who would respond favourably to a particular marketing strategy and the main ones are discussed below.

Market segmentation variables

The process of selecting the market segment, or segments, to be served starts with the identification of potential segments. The choice of segmentation criteria is vitally important, yet its significance is often underestimated. It is the choice of criteria that will determine how the firm chooses to pursue its market opportunities and the means by which it does so. Once potential segments have been identified, they need to be reviewed in terms of their relevance for further evaluation. Finally, they are assessed on the basis of their fit with the firm's core business and the likelihood that electing to serve them will meet the firm's financial or other objectives.

As an example, Novo Nordisk Service Partners, a Danish provider of facilities management services, carried out its segmentation on the basis of a detailed market analysis. The company found that this analysis provided valuable insights about how large and small companies among its potential customers viewed the prospect of outsourcing in related areas. Figure 3.3 indicates the nature of the market analysis carried out by this facility's management service provider.

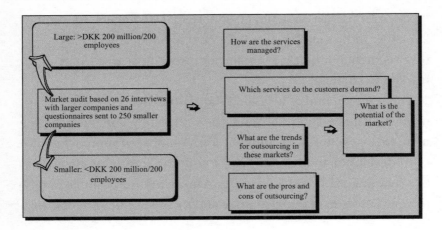

Figure 3.3 – Understanding the market potential.

In some instances, firms segment a market on the basis of just one variable, typically the industry (e.g., forestry or oil drilling), or the size of the customer (e.g., turnover or number of employees). With some reservations we observe that this may be appropriate for certain broad decisions such as the type of product offerings to be made. For the development of a comprehensive marketing strategy, however, it is necessary to take into account a wide variety of variables, relevant to the many decisions associated with the strategy.

The starting point for market segmentation should be the identification of all possible segmentation variables. Generally, these variables are divided into 'macro' and 'micro' categories. *Macro variables* are those that focus on the buying organization, and include size, location, industry, market level (e.g., OEM or end user) and the end market served by potential customers. *Micro variables* are those that focus on the decision-making unit and include individual characteristics of buyers, decision criteria, type of purchase situation, benefits sought and perceived importance of the purchase. Figure 3.4 provides a list of possible variables and possible categories for segmenting the computer market.

Segmentation criteria	Examples from the IT industry
Industry:	Banking, retailing, manufacturing, shipping
Application:	General purpose, process control, business computation, scientific research
Geography:	USA, Japan, France
Size:	Large multinational, large national, medium size, small
Buying behaviour:	Sealed bid from multiple sources, negotiated bid from sole source
Buying culture:	Innovator, follower, OEMs, value-added resellers
Buyer strategy:	Defender, prospector, analyzer reactor
Benefits sought:	Hardware characteristics, software availability, service

Figure 3.4 – Possible variables and categories for IT industry market segmentation.

Although many segmentation variables are reasonably obvious, some are not. Rolm Corporation, for instance, when it introduced the first digital switch for use in telephone switching, included the attitudes of state public utility commissions in the United States toward AT&T as one of its segmentation variables. It elected to enter markets only in those states in which it felt that the regulatory bodies would favour increased competition for AT&T.

Segmentation approaches

The most widely cited segmentation approach is a *two-stage segmentation approach.* This approach starts with macro-segmentation that is based on the characteristics of the buying organization. Within the macro-segments, the focus of attention is the characteristics of the particular decision-making unit. This exercise needs to be carried out with care. In particular, it is important to remember that many micro-segmentation variables are found in more than one macro-segment.

A *nested, or multi-stage, approach* utilizes a number of categories. The analysis might start with the outer nests – the general, easily observable segmentation variables – and then might move toward the inner nests – the more specific, subtle, or hard-to-assess variables. For instance, the analysis may dictate that we move from Geography to Industry to Application to purchasing approach to functional decision makers. Some caveats need to be observed regarding the use of this approach. The notion of starting with the outer nests is based on the premise that they are easier to work with, not that there is a rigid sense of hierarchy to the analysis.

Most recently, a *three-stage needs-based approach* for segmenting outsourcing markets has been proposed. This approach is designed to identify potential early adopters of new technologies, using organizational needs revealed by actual purchasing behaviour, based on the assumption that past purchasing behaviour is a good predictor of future behaviour. The first stage is macro-segmentation, designed to delineate firms that have broadly similar needs and to reduce the total market to generally manageable segments. The second stage is micro-segmentation, to further segment the macro-segments based on benefits and/or needs. Despite the fact that customer needs are the most logical segmentation base, they can only provide managers with part of the information necessary for target market selection and development of marketing strategy. Hence, the third stage is to further describe micro-segments in terms that can be directly linked to specific elements of marketing strategy.

These segmentation approaches give rise to a number of considerations that should be kept in mind when conducting a segmentation study:

1. *Segmentation should always be guided by an objective.* As potential segments are considered, their usefulness should be tested in terms of their relevance to the particular aspect of

marketing strategy under consideration. In some instances, the purpose will be to develop a complete marketing strategy involving all elements of the marketing mix. We would expect such a study to extensively describe potential segments in terms of many segmentation variables. In other instances, the purpose might simply be to develop an advertising campaign with messages varied to most effectively communicate with significant groups of customers, or to develop a set of pricing strategies that take into account variations in pricing sensitivity of groups of customers. We would expect such a study might be more limited in its use of segmentation variables.

2. *Segmentation requires both rigour and creativity.* Secondary data abound on the size of markets based on geographical dimensions, Standard Industrial Classification codes, or other classifications. Additional secondary data based on past order histories or other forms of marketing intelligence usually exist in company files. In many instances, these data lend themselves to various statistical methodologies such as cluster or factor analysis. There is, however, no set list of variables that definitively identifies a market segment. As indicated in the Rolm example, the creative use of variables enhances insights for marketing strategy.

3. *The segmentation is, or should be, iterative.* Identification of a micro-segment in one macro-segment should be followed by consideration of its existence in others. Segmentation on the basis of needs or benefits is particularly likely to cut across several macro-segments.

Criteria for initial screening

The search for market segments is likely to reveal several segments of varying attractiveness. Some segments may not be real in the sense that they are not measurable. Others may not be reachable. Before embarking on extensive evaluation of potential market segments, it is advisable to test their usefulness against the following broad characteristics:

1. *Measurability.* We can hypothesize about a number of variables that might influence how buyers respond to various outsourcing marketing strategies. However, unless they are measurable, it would be impossible to use them to estimate the size of a particular segment.
2. *Unique response.* For a segment to be meaningful, it must respond differentially from another segment to at least one element of the marketing mix, i.e., product/service offering, positioning, pricing, communication, or channel choice.
3. *Sufficiency.* The aggregate demand of the customers making up the segment must be sufficient to cover marketing costs. Anticipated sales, taking into account not only the size of the segment but also its expected market share, must generate sufficient contribution to margin in order to cover the added cost of a specialized outsourcing marketing programme.
4. *Accessibility.* There must be some basis on which we can identify, and hence reach, a particular segment. With new outsourcing services we may wish to reach customers who are innovators. Unless there is some characteristic that identifies the customer as an innovator, we are not likely to be able to reach this segment.

Evaluating potential segments

Of the identified segments that are real and reachable, some will represent a better profit opportunity or a better fit for the company than others. The ultimate objective in selecting a segment is profitability, but there are many other considerations. Below are suggested questions that need to be answered before finalizing a decision to target a particular segment:

- How well do the requirements to successfully compete in the segment fit our distinctive competence? For example, does our sales force have the necessary skills to deal with a segment in which intense negotiation characterizes the purchasing process?
- How well does the segment capitalize on the firm's current position? Can it be reached, for instance, with our present delivery mechanisms?
- What are the growth prospects for the segment, either long term or short term? Do they match its sales growth objectives?
- Are sales likely to be cyclical? If so, can we adjust our operations and marketing efforts to both the ups and the downs of demand in the market in general or for our current clients?
- Does a particular segment exhibit enough difference in response to justify its treatment as a separate segment with requirements for a separate outsourcing marketing programme? Would differences in buying behaviour, for instance, require separate sales forces and operations, or are the buying power differences within the range that would be expected and that could be accommodated reasonably within normal workloads of the sales force and supply chain?
- Assuming a successful outsourcing marketing programme for a particular segment, would it be defensible against competitive attack? How likely is it that a competitor could match a particular offering and, if it could do so, within what period of time would its offering become available? Are buyers likely to be loyal to a pioneer? What would be the switching costs for customers to change to a different supplier?

- Is there the capacity within the firm's resources to implement a marketing plan that effectively reaches and serves the segment or segments?
- Will targeting this segment or segments lead the company in the direction its managers want it to go?

The final test of the attractiveness of a particular segment is the ability of the firm to develop an implementable marketing strategy.

There are some additional issues in segmentation. For example, selecting a segment goes beyond simply identifying a potentially attractive segment. How the segment is defined may significantly influence competitor evaluation or future initiatives. Segments emerge, or become clearer, over the lifecycle, raising issues of timing. Finding niches or segments that the firm can dominate to the exclusion of competitors is a special consideration as is vertical segmentation. Finally, changes in the external environment constantly introduce new possibilities for segmentation variables as is particularly evident in considering opportunities outside home country markets.

Defining the market

Although the segmentation process is used primarily to improve the likelihood of a favourable response to a given outsourcing marketing strategy from a carefully selected set of customers, it should also be recognized that the decision as to which segment, or combination of segments, to target defines the denominator in market share calculations. An excessively narrow definition of the served market - a restrictive geographic definition, for instance - can result in overstating the firm's market share and incorrectly estimating the firm's competitive position. In the early stages of CT scanners, GE defined its market as hospitals only in the United States, leading it to conclude that it had a dominant position, based on a 60% share of market. Redefining its market as hospitals world-wide dropped its market share to less than 20%, leading to a signifi-cant re-evaluation of its position. Subsequently, GE has moved into managing outsourced CT scanning operations, which again is a re-definition of the market. Segments, therefore, should be defined to include not just the customers that the firm currently attempts to serve but also those customers with similar wants and needs who are being served by the firm's competitors, in both domestic and foreign markets.

Timing, niche markets and global considerations

In the introductory and early growth stages of the lifecycle for the solution, customer needs are not necessarily clear or easily defin-able. When solution concepts are new, early acceptance by some buyers may not indicate true market potential and buyers may have little in the way of experience to develop definitive opinions about product features. As solution concepts become better understood, new groups of buyers may emerge. Early commitment to one seg-ment, therefore, has the potential to reduce the ability to serve other segments.

As more buyers gain experience, a better basis for specific need definitions is established and the late growth and mature stages of the solution lifecycle are characterized by the emergence of segments with differentiated needs. Failure to develop specialized offerings for these segments may result in competitive disadvantage.

When products are beyond the introductory stage of the solution lifecycle, we expect to find several firms competing for a share in the market. Within market segments, therefore, we frequently find firms looking for groups of customers, or niches, for which a very specialized marketing strategy can establish a position not easily duplicated by competitors. Looking for such niches does not guarantee that they will be found. There generally is only room for one player to reach minimum efficient scale, which makes the importance of clear positioning a significant issue in the segment choice. Segments can be evaluated, however, on the basis of customer loyalty to pioneers and switching costs. More particularly, effective competitor analysis can evaluate the likelihood of competitor response or the timing of such response.

Despite country differences, the nature of business marketing with heavy emphasis on functionality is such that foreign sales have long been important for most firms. In the market for solutions, however, the need for local adaptation and presence is vital. Gaining global scalability is difficult to achieve – much consideration has to be given to strategy definition and roll-out.

The traditional approach to foreign markets has been to segment on the basis of countries. Few segmentation variables would seem more straightforward. An atlas easily provides the basis for delineation of segments. In most instances, language, laws and currencies vary as a function of national boundaries. As we have previously described, business customs also may vary, sometimes on a regional basis and sometimes on a national basis. As a result, there has been a tendency to develop marketing strategies for individual countries – the so-called polycentric approach operating on the assumption that each country is so different as to require a unique marketing strategy.

The obvious differences among countries frequently obscure the many similarities that make a case for global or regional strategies. Today many firms are developing strategies that are essentially common across countries except for language and currency denomination. Firms such as Johnson Controls are rolling facility management concepts out internationally, but with relevant local adaptations for international clients.

Sales force management in a changed environment

As a result of the emergence of new forms of relationships between suppliers and buyers – the growth of alliances and network relations – traditional sales procedures and traditional sales force skills are becoming obsolete. In the new environment of outsourcing and marketing of total solutions to buyers for whom this option is strategically valuable, it is vital for managers to use different strategies and tactics for sales force management. The significance of new management approaches is rising swiftly in line with the rapidly escalating interest of business executives in building relationships with other companies in order to compete effectively in turbulent and rapidly changing global markets. Because most companies lack an accurate perspective on this change and its repercussions for sales force management, they continue to develop their sales forces in the image of the previous generation of successful salespeople.

Changes to the marketplace and to marketing have highly significant implications for sales force management. Today buyers work with fewer suppliers than in the past and we see many reflections of this change. *Key accounts, strategic accounts, national accounts* and *partner accounts* are some of the terms used to refer to new forms of sales force activities. As we have discussed previously, buyer interest in greater flexibility and responsiveness in order to supply increasingly complex products and services is leading to a heightened emphasis on total solutions. Meeting these diverse requirements calls for greater knowledge depth, greater technological competence and greater response capability. The full implications of such changes for the marketing process and hence for the marketing organization, although not particularly well understood at present, appear to require substantial reorientation of managerial thinking about sales force development.

As with products, a sales force has a lifecycle. At some point the sales arising from the sales organization's activities will level off as markets become saturated, or as competitors arise, or as traditional sales strategies become ineffective. Any of these forms of obsolescence requires that companies have the ability to change. The adoption and implementation of new business management processes are essential for targeting, selling and servicing the evolving needs of customers, both old and new, in an effective manner, especially in the complex relationship environment of outsourcing.

Sales force development for supplying total solutions

The provision of total solutions may fail because of implementation problems. Although much research has been focused on strategic choices about whether to outsource or not and what exactly to outsource, rather limited attention has been devoted to implementation issues, most notably in terms of establishing the correct interface between marketing strategy and sales force activities.

An effective marketing strategy should define the role and the expected behaviour of the sales force so that appropriate strategies can be devised (Kashani, 1984). This role definition and the definition of expected behaviour must then be mirrored in the Sales Force Management Policy and the daily performance management of the sales force in the field. Change may necessitate an evaluation of the firm's recruiting and selection policy as well as its training and reward processes. On this basis we suggest that the development of the sales force should focus specifically on the delivery of the planned strategy for providing the total solution.

How can sales managers effect change in their sales force personnel when the marketing strategy is radically altered to supply total solutions to outsourcing buyers? A central issue concerns the differences between selling products, as in the case of traditional sales, and selling total solutions that involve complex selling and facilities management. First, there is a need for coordination or teamwork to enable the company to identify and act upon opportunities. Second, there is a need for commitment to enable the company to marshal the effort, initiative and cooperation necessary for coordinated action and third, there is a need for competencies that are relevant to the changed operating environment if employees are to work effectively as a team to solve problems. These three interrelated factors are beneficial to any company trying to coordinate strategic decisions regarding marketing and implementation.

In some instances a company may decide that it is preferable from a cost, or other, perspective to outsource its sales force activities. Service providers of sales force services may offer a solution that is more financially attractive than in-house training of sales force personnel. The example of AMS (Advanced Marketing Solutions), an American company that specializes in providing high-value marketing and sales support to clients, illustrates this point. Its 'outsourced sales force solutions' are promoted as having some key benefits for customers:

> AMS demonstrates value through small pilot programmes as well as ultra-efficient large-scale programmes that expand based on client success and approval. With an increasing return on investment, clients can explore a growing number of scalable outsourcing options. AMS pricing for ongoing programmes is typically 50% variable (driven by clients based on marketing response volume and programme requirements) and 50% fixed to have an AMS team available.
>
> (http://www.internetleads.com/why.shtml)

Building sales force capabilities

Sales force training is an important function, particularly when a company moves from offering straight product sales to selling solutions and facilities management contracts. Although the objectives of sales training may vary from firm to firm, there is some agreement on broad goals – to increase productivity, improve morale, lower turnover, improve customer relations and produce better management of time and territory (Churchill *et al.*, 1985). However, there are numerous problems that companies face when trying to implement sales training programmes. In a survey by Peterson (1990), sales managers were asked to identify the problems that they faced when trying to introduce sales training programmes. The top five obstacles identified by the 297 respondents are the following:

- Lack of dedication by top management to sales training
- Inadequate funding of sales training programmes
- Apathy among salespeople about sales training
- Resentment about the time commitment required for sales training
- Resistance to the changes suggested by sales training programmes.

This rather negative perspective of sales training raises an important question: What can managers do to overcome these problems? Often managers expect that sales training will be a panacea for all of the company's sales problems. Frequently they fail to see sales training as an investment that pays future dividends and not simply a cost of doing business. How then does a supplier of total solutions develop competitive advantage with its sales force? Below are four suggestions for effective sales force development planning that are based on strategies for competing on the basis of capabilities (Stalk *et al.*, 1992):

1. *Regard the sales process as one of the processes that is a building block of corporate strategy.*
   Processes, not products or markets, are the building blocks of a company's strategy. By highlighting the sales process as a key

corporate process the activities are more likely to receive serious attention from busy managers.

2. *Focus on transforming the sales process into strategic capabilities that will consistently provide superior value to customers.*
   The sales force can become a source of competitive advantage when it focuses on the development of capabilities that can consistently provide superior value to customers.

3. *Invest in the development of a support infrastructure that will transcend the fragmentation of traditional business units and functions to help the sales force create strategic capabilities.*
   The sales force must be positioned as part of a larger business team to bring in the collective organizational wisdom required for total solutions.

4. *Position the CEO/MD as the champion of the development of an excellent sales force because capabilities cross functions in the company.*
   The support of the CEO or MD is essential to gain the interest and support of all of the relevant company functions as required for development of the strategic capabilities essential for the provision of total solutions.

Pressures on competitiveness arising from global sourcing, reductions by major customers in numbers of suppliers and other problems triggered by low economic growth add urgency to the search for greater effectiveness and superior performance in selling operations (Hise and Reid, 1994; Babakus *et al.*, 1997). In the case of suppliers of total solutions these pressures have led to changes in marketing and sales force management based on new forms of relationships with buyers.

Summary

In the retooling of marketing and the sales force specifically for the provision of outsourcing solutions several key points should be emphasized. First, because the fundamental objective of marketing strategy is to meet customer wants and needs more effectively than competitors at a profit to the firm, the pressures to aggregate segments for greater economies of scale/critical mass, or to further segment markets to better meet customer needs/better respond to competitor threats, are continuous. Second, market segmentation decisions must be accompanied by decisions to commit the necessary organizational resources, talents and energies without which even the best market segmentation strategy is unlikely to succeed. Third, the process of market segmentation is both analytical and creative and also dynamic – segmentation processes need to take changing customer needs into account. Finally, retooling the sales force to provide total solutions involves clear recognition of the management consequences of the new partnership relationships between sellers and their buyers – partnerships that fundamentally make traditional approaches to both sales force training and sales force management obsolete.

References

Babakus, E., Cravens, D. W., Grant, K., Ingram, T. N. and LaForge, R. 1997. Investigating the relationships between sales management control, sales territory design, salesperson performance, and sales organisation effectiveness, *International Journal of Research in Marketing,* Vol. 13, No. 4, pp. 345–363.

Churchill, G., Ford, N. and Wright, O. 1985. *Sales force management: Planning, implementation and control:* 4th edition, Irwin, Homewood, IL.

Hayes, H. M., Jenster, P. V. and Aaby, N.-E. 1996. *Business marketing – A global perspective*, Irwin, Chicago.

Hise, R. T. and Reid, E. L. 1994. Improving the performance of the industrial sales force in the 1990s, *Industrial Marketing Management,* Vol. 28, pp. 553–564.

Kashani, K. 1984. Managing the transition from marketing strategy to sales force action, *Journal of Sales Management*, Vol. 1, No. 2, pp. 21–26.

Peterson, R. T. 1990. What makes sales training programmes successful? *Training and Development Journal*, Vol. 44, No. 8, pp. 59–64.

Stalk, G., Evans, P. and Shulman, L. 1992. Competing on capabilities: The new rules of corporate strategy, *Harvard Business Review*, March–April, Vol. 70, No. 2, pp. 57–69.

Managing buyer/ supplier relationships

4

Introduction

In this chapter we examine outsourcing relationships first from the perspective of a supplier and then follow with the perspective of a buyer. For these discussions we are looking at outsourcing when it is no longer an incremental activity. These relationships present challenges to both the supplier and the buyer. For the supplier the main concerns can be broken into three main categories – challenges related to the necessary competencies, challenges related to managing the entry phase and challenges related to running the contract. For the buyer the challenges can be grouped according to the four major activities – pre-bid reconnaissance activities, key supplier identification, contract awarding and contract management. The three cases included in this chapter – Timex Dundee, IBM Denmark and the UK Driver and Vehicle Licensing Agency – illustrate a number of the key points.

The challenges for suppliers

As outsourcing contracts become more complex and more critical, both the buyer and the supplier have to change. Researchers at IMD developed a 'step model' based on research into the automotive industry as supplier and buyer move into an ever-closer relationship.

The significant observation was that for every step the supplier had to make, there had to be a step made by the buyer.

The example given was the outsourcing of cockpit modules from VW-Skoda to Siemens-Aledart. Initially the contract was straight-forward outsourcing, with the key task for the supplier being con-formance to specifications. Skoda's motivation was cost reduction, and its main task was to make sure that it received the correct as-semblies in line with the contract. The supplier had to be successful in meeting the specifications. This was Step 1.

Step 2 saw the supplier taking on the logistics responsibility of working with the large number of suppliers who provided the com-ponents that went into assembling the cockpit. This step is about coordinating schedules and tying component suppliers to JIT deliv-eries in order to minimize inventories. The main additional task on top of conformance for Siemens-Aledart is to ensure that it can meet the ever-changing requirements of Skoda's production on a JIT basis. Skoda, in turn, has to simplify its infrastructure as the relationship moves from cost reduction to an operational focus.

By Step 3 Siemens-Aledart was able to work to capture a larger slice of the available pie by seeking different ways to maximize its gain while still preserving functionality. Figure 4.1 suggests that this result might be achieved through backwards integration into the manufacture of one or more components. What is significant is that to make this work Skoda has to reconfigure some of its own competency requirements to enable it to take a strategic fo-cus, in relation to both its own activities and those provided by the supplier.

In the final step in Figure 4.1 Siemens-Aledart took responsi-bility for design of the cockpit, achieving seeking cost benefits through breakthrough actions. This step could not have been effec-tive without Skoda wanting a genuine strategic partnership so that

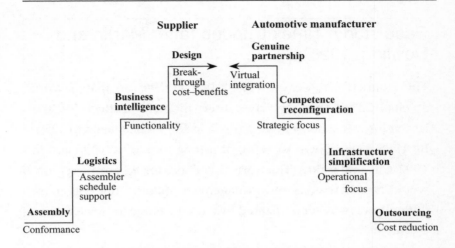

Figure 4.1 – Competence development and enhancement through partnering in the auto industry. (After Tom Vollman and Carlos Cordon, Outsourcing Project Workshop Presentation, 2000).

the supplier and the buyer were sharing information and knowledge, and working toward common goals.

Each step on this ladder brings different management challenges, and even the lowest step is light years away from the antagonistic relationship of traditional purchasing. Each step has to result in a win–win situation and both parties have to gain as a result. This outcome cannot be achieved unless both parties organize and manage themselves in a very different way.

The first challenge for suppliers comes when it decides to seek outsourcing business and this challenge increases as it moves from what may be an incremental activity at the traditional level of our Figure 1.1 to the very different situation of the more complex requirements. We suggest that the serious supplier needs to think of the outsourcing activity as a business in its own right as many have done. The Timex case study gives an illustration of a situation where this did not happen.

Case study: Timex Dundee (after Martin and Dowling, 1995)

The Dundee plants were established in 1947 to manufacture mechanical watches for Timex internationally. In the 1970s the labour force reached a peak of 6000: in 1975 it had fallen to 4200. By 1985 it was down to 1000, dropping to 580 by 1990 and in 1992 was under 500. This sort of decline, for whatever reason, would tax HRM skills and management abilities, but was more difficult as it was accompanied by a total change in the activities of the business.

Until the 1970s, Timex Dundee with its three plants was a manufacturing satellite of Timex internationally. Its task was to produce watches under a cost leadership strategy, with all product development centred in the USA, manufacturing long runs of mass-produced watches that carried reasonably high margins. The evidence suggests that it did this job well and was a cash generator for Timex as a whole.

Historically, Timex Dundee faced an aggressive trade union and the story of Dundee was of adversarial relations, with a history of compromise and accommodation, anything to prevent disruption of production that would have affected Timex markets throughout the world. Management appeared to manage its industrial relations with only short-term objectives in mind. As a result, the union became very powerful, not only in wage bargaining, but also in taking over considerable control of how labour was organized to undertake the various activities in the factory. In this respect the local management was typical of many other organizations in the UK at the time in that even communication by management to employees passed by default through the filter of the shop stewards. During this period, and until about

1980, Timex had a reputation as a good employer, offering career prospects, training and good working conditions.

Timex appears to have been taken by surprise at the international decline of mechanical watches and their replacement by electronics. When it did respond, it set up new plants in other countries to make watches using the new technology and the importance of Dundee to the international watch marketing strategy withered to nothing. Nevertheless, there was a sentimental attachment to the Dundee operation at the top of Timex USA and a willingness to try to maintain an activity there, although not for the reasons that it was originally established.

As mechanical watch volumes declined, the Dundee plants had moved into subcontracting assembly of electronic products, initially the Sinclair ZX computer and a Japanese-designed camera. This incremental strategy appeared to be a logical way of making up for the undercapacity utilization and to be compatible with overall Timex expertise because the parent company was involved in manufacturing related products.

Nonetheless, Timex Dundee suffered a triple blow. The Sinclair ZX computer manufacture was transferred to IBM, the camera operations moved to Japan and the remaining watch manufacture was relocated to France. These changes resulted in compulsory redundancies of 1900 people in 1983 and a worker sit-in aimed at preventing the transfer of work out of Dundee. Management fought the sit-in and insisted on the compulsory redundancies and on changes in flexibility for those who remained.

Discussions took place between the American and local managements about the future of the Dundee operations. Although it was recognized that the Dundee cost structure was too high, the decision was taken to keep the personnel employed as contract assemblers of electronic equipment. A new general manager was brought in by the American management team to strengthen local management's electronics knowledge. The business continued to develop in contract manufacturing and related services for original equipment manufacturers in the electronics industry and by the late 1980s the company had secured a place in the electronics industry.

During the 1980s the electronics markets expanded rapidly. Timex invested substantially in new plant and by 1993 were one of the big six contract electronic assemblers in the UK. Redundancies, mainly voluntary, occurred throughout the period, as the company strived to remove its cost disadvantage of 20–30% compared with competitors. IBM was one of the major customers and had installed electronic control systems that gave it instant access to production information. Dundee managers had little influence over sourcing or scheduling as these decisions were taken by IBM, who also controlled price and conformance to specifications.

In 1990 an attempt was made to change the culture of the organization in the *Fresh Start* Change Programme. This programme was initiated from the USA and its aims were to break with past industrial relations traditions, to support more redundancies and to concentrate all production into one factory. There was a buy-out of some of the restrictive contract terms. Employees who survived the redundancy received a payment of £2000 to accept the new contract terms. In addition, a share ownership scheme was introduced.

In June 1991 a new general manager was recruited to run the Dundee plant and turn it around, in what was frankly described as 'the last throw of the dice'. He introduced a number of well-received efficiencies, but did not establish rapport with the union officials and representatives. They saw him as an aggressive dictator who saw every concession they made as their weakness.

This atmosphere was hardly conducive to the continuation of the *Fresh Start* initiative. The closing events in the drama occurred in late 1992 when IBM cut back on its scheduled requirements. Local management developed a cost-cutting scheme in conjunction with two USA-based vice presidents involving lay-offs and wage reduction. Initially the workers rejected the scheme and went on strike, then they accepted under protest. The general manager said that grudging commitment was not good enough and sacked 340 workers whom he replaced with non-union workers from outside the district. This episode led to aggressive mass picketing over a four-month period. Ultimately, a peace plan was put to the strikers, involving even worse terms than they had previously accepted. This proposal was rejected. The general manager resigned suddenly, and the US management decided to close the plant. There is now no Timex operation in Dundee. (Hussey, 2002)

The initial motivation for getting into contract assembly was for overhead spreading and labour retention by making use of spare capacity. Although it is possible to sympathize with these actions, we should also query whether they formed a sound basis for a new business activity. The second phase followed similar reasoning, except that now contract assembly for external customers was to be the business.

There was a belief that the company had the necessary manufacturing strengths, expertise and experience to succeed in contract assembly. Because local management was totally focused on manufacture, there were no insights from functions such as product development and marketing, and the only external thinking came from US managers who were blinkered by their perceptions of the role of Dundee operations as an anomaly in the current international strategy.

It is interesting to speculate about whether the company might still have succeeded had it related its strengths and competence to the requirements of the market they were going to concentrate on. There is a vital difference between taking on some contract assembly activities to help absorb the overheads and retain skilled workers (the Sinclair situation) and running a total business that is wholly focused on such contract work.

The competency requirements of the new business included:

- Great flexibility, with the ability to change economically between products
- Ability to work as an extension of the customers' businesses
- Competitive cost base to enable success in a different type of business
- Dealing with greater unpredictability of products and volumes
- Marketing and sales as all customers would be external to Timex
- Continuous attention to technical skills, to keep up to date with new or different products
- Building added value into client relationships.

These competencies appeared to be absent at the outset. The cost problem was known, and additional top management knowledge and experience were brought in, as described, some investment was made and there were efforts to increase the flexibility of working methods. What was absent was an exhaustive analysis of all the human resource issues and needs and development of a human resource strategy as an integral part of the business strategy. At this stage a hard-nosed examination should have been made of whether it would even be possible to bring about the necessary changes, particularly changes in culture. We might also ask whether it would ever have been possible to succeed in this type of business given the industrial relations climate and prevailing culture.

The culture change programme, which one could fairly argue was at least 10 years too late, was probably doomed from the start. It was driven by American managers who had little understanding of, or empathy with, the culture they were trying to change, and many local managers were not committed to the process. With hindsight the appearance is more of a one-off intervention rather than a step in a carefully thought-out HR strategy. The costs of the change programme and other restructuring contributed to accumulated losses of £10 million between 1987 and 1993.

Unless the supplier can get the fundamentals of its own business in order, it has little chance of long-term success, and moving to a win–win situation may be impossible. Our second case study indicates some of the problems IBM overcame in its efforts to build a total solutions and facilities management business.

When IBM spun off much of its hardware and components manufacturing, in the mid-1990s, it showed how the reconfiguration of a company's manufacturing strategy could advance an overall strategic shift. Only after IBM had redefined its core – e-business services and solutions, research and design, and semiconductor architecture and manufacturing – did it reconstruct its supply chain, thus creating, in the end, a different company. Ownership of computer hardware and components manufacturing is essentially nil at today's IBM, but the company's financial performance has soared – from losses of £8.1 billion in 1993 to net income of £8.09 billion in 2000. The return on invested capital rose similarly, from −5.7 percent in 1993 to 15.3 percent in 2000. (Doig *et al.*, 2001)

Case Study: IBM Denmark

Business forces are driving the outsourcing of IT. In the early 1990s outsourcing decisions were mainly driven by customers' wishes to reduce costs. By the end of the decade the key driver was the customers' lack of in-house expertise. When individual companies have difficulties in keeping up to speed with developments, outsourcing becomes a more strategic option.

IBM had to determine how to approach the market and how it might combine its various activities. It had to continue offering products to those customers who wanted them, while at the same time organizing to meet the needs of those who required services. The company defined the requirements of service customers as:

- knowledge and expertise,
- value for money,
- speed and efficiency,
- a trusting relationship, and
- solutions to business problems.

In the 1980s IBM did not possess the skills to deliver services on a continuous basis. It lacked the capability to attack the entire value chain, although customers wanted it to have this capability. It also had to avoid having the links in the value chain operate too independently.

Between 1988 and 1991 its activities related to each branch of the value chain were seen as separate businesses. For example, sales forces, application solutions, systems engineering and consultancy were all viewed as separate businesses. In 1991 all the service departments were pulled from the existing structure into a new activity – the IBM Consultancy Group.

Among the many challenges was developing competencies in project management, which required a major educational effort. However, this was only one of many internal issues that had to be tackled. Incentive systems had to be changed because they were inappropriate for the focus of the organization. Methods of reporting how employees spent their time had to be developed and applied. Without these data estimating costs for bids for new contracts would have been a matter of guesswork and any contract cost control would have been defective.

To make the sort of shift that IBM made requires a mix of sound analysis and creative strategic thinking. Organizations like IBM with an established reputation and strong technical competence have real advantages in developing what is a new type of business. It is customer needs that should drive how a modern outsourcing supplier is created, or reshaped, from existing strengths. If this element is missing from the planning, the result can well be failure. Timex appeared to have been driven by the facilities and competencies it already had. IBM, with much greater strengths, knew that it had to reinvent its activities if it was to obtain a continuation of its record of satisfied customers.

Research by Ozanne (2000), quoted by Doig *et al.* (2001), shows that suppliers have to work hard to satisfy customers. Between one-fifth and one-quarter of all outsourcing relationships fail within two years. Only a half last longer than five years. The supplier or the buyer can cause failure, but when 70% of respondents to the survey believed that their suppliers did not understand them and that the relationship delivered high costs and poor service, there is a strong indication that many suppliers have not given thought to the fundamentals.

Supplier Challenge 1 – The need for additional competencies

The IBM case illustrated one approach to developing essential new competencies. The need for project management was tackled through extensive management education. Recruitment is another method. There are three others that are commonly used: alliances, acquisitions and outsourcing.

Alliances

One result of the modern outsourcing movement is that for complex projects the additional competencies have often been secured by alliances. This strategy may do more than provide scarce skills and other assets: it may also enable the partners to benefit from each other's reputation. The examples we give also illustrate one of the weaknesses of alliances, namely that changes in the ownership of one of the parties can lead to problems. For example, Price-waterhouseCoopers (PWC) had an alliance with Hewlett Packard Compaq that rapidly crumbled when IBM acquired the consulting arm of PWC in 2002.

In January 2002 *Management Consultants' News Direct* reported that IBM Global Services had

> partnered with VeriSign to provide digital trust services to 5000 of the largest companies world-wide in an alliance which could generate revenues of more than $1 billion over the next three years. . . . IBM Global Services will work with VeriSign Consulting Services and its network of global affiliates to provide managed services and support for companies using public key infrastructure (PKI) technology and digital signatures to secure e-business application. The service will integrate on VeriSign's managed PKI infrastructure services and technology and IBM's Tivoli Policy Director, security management and access control software.

PWC had made a similar alliance with Entrust a short while before.

There are numerous examples, particularly in the IT field, of outsourcing suppliers building alliances of this type. Alliances are not easy to manage. If the supplier is moving down this route, success requires a number of specific skills and competencies.

Acquisitions

Outsourcing suppliers have also been building capabilities by acquisition. This approach may be undertaken to add particular competencies, or to develop global capacity. Although this may be a sensible strategy, it is also a very difficult one. There has been a long history of research into acquisition success and failure with repeated confirmation that around half of all acquisitions fail. Recent research by KPMG (2001), using shareholder value as the criterion, found that only 30% of acquisitions increased value, 31% destroyed it and the rest did neither.

This is not the place to discuss in detail why acquisitions so often fail (see Hussey, 1999 for some clues). However, failure may occur at any, or at every, point along the acquisition process from an ill-conceived strategy to a failure in post-purchase implementation. In between may lie overpayment for the acquisition, insufficient knowledge about the company being acquired and absence of a post-purchase implementation plan. Suppliers following the acquisition route should not see it as an easy option and, as with alliances, it does call for some particular management capabilities.

We mentioned above the IBM acquisition of the consultancy side of PWC. IBM acquired this business just before its planned spin-off to PWC. Its plan was to trade under the unusual name of 'Monday'. This acquisition certainly boosted the consulting strength of IBM and the general opinion is that the purchase was a bargain. Integration of acquired consulting firms is notoriously difficult, partly because there is often a clash of cultures and partly because styles of consulting may differ with what appears on the surface to be the same but is in reality very different. The best consultants are also highly mobile. The acquisition is being accompanied by a reduction of employee numbers, which although no doubt essential is hardly the best start to integration.

Outsourcing

Supplier firms may also find it desirable to outsource. In such instances the supplier company becomes an outsourcing buyer. This step may be taken as a means of adding competencies, or for cost reduction and/or service improvement as illustrated in Figure 4.1.

It is possible to argue that alliances are also a form of outsourcing. The main difference is that in the alliances the partners are sharing some of the bid costs and are also bearing the risks of not obtaining the contract as well as presumably sharing the profits. Outsourcing may fit the patterns discussed in Chapters 1 and 2 and may fall into any one of our four categories in Figure 1.1. The points we make later in this chapter about buyers may also be relevant to some suppliers.

It is also possible to outsource labour requirements, by using either contract employees or temporary agencies. This approach may be forced on the supplier by shortages of particular types of people, or it may be as a means of achieving flexibility to enable prompt adjustments to differences in supply and demand. One example, which was mentioned in Chapter 2, also illustrates the dangers. In the UK railway track and signal inspection and maintenance are outsourced to several specialist organizations serving defined geographical areas that, in turn, outsource much of their labour requirements in the way described above. Not all these temporary hires have railway experience, although many will be from civil engineering. Following recent accidents that were attributed in the media to poor maintenance, a widely held belief developed that many of these personnel were badly trained and were, therefore, incapable of doing a good job. Whether this impression is true or false, it is damaging to the companies concerned.

Supplier Challenge 2 – Managing the entry phase

The relationship between the supplier and the buyer begins at the entry phase during which both parties have to interact. The entry phase covers the period from initial discussions with the buyer about a real project to the award of the contract. Large outsourcing contracts are usually complex and normally the bidding process is competitive. We have concentrated on these aspects of the entry phase.

The supplier has many issues to consider, some of which relate only to its own business and some of which are of critical importance to both parties. We will look more closely at the buyer side later in the chapter, although some aspects can be deduced from examining the supplier view.

In addition to the insights gained from the outsourcing research programme of Copenhagen Business School, we found Hodson (2002) a very useful aid to our thinking.

Assessing the business opportunity

Bidding can be a very expensive process. Before getting involved in the expense of bid preparation, the supplier will want to assess the opportunity. This exercise is partly to determine whether the contract, if won, is likely to bring satisfaction to the client, partly to get a preliminary feel of the risks involved and partly to assess the chances of winning the contract. The wise supplier will be ready to walk away from the opportunity at this stage before it is involved in the costs of a bid that is likely to fail:

- *Is the buyer financially stable?* Outsourcing contracts are designed to last for a reasonable length of time. If it appears that the buyer is likely to have cash problems, the effects on the supplier could be catastrophic. There is always a commercial risk of this type, but it is clearly greater with some buyers than with others.
- *Does the buyer know what it wants to achieve?* If there is confusion about expectations, the final outcome is likely to be

disappointment and it may also be very difficult to manage the contract if the buyer is perpetually changing its mind about what it wants.

- *What are the motives behind the invitation to bid?* We have explored the motives for outsourcing elsewhere and these, in part, relate to the above point. However, there is another aspect. Is the invitation to bid put out so that the buying organization can claim to have gone through a competitive bid process although there is already a preferred bidder? In the latter half of 2002 a number of firms refused the invitation to bid for a large outsourcing contract for the UK's Inland Revenue because they believed that another organization, which was already working on a related contract, was the preferred bidder.

- *Has the buyer prepared a business case for the outsourcing?* Apart from helping to clarify what the buyer wants, the business case also provides essential information on assumptions. In the Passport Agency example the business case provided the volume forecasts on which the bid was based.

- *Has the buyer allocated an appropriate amount of funds for the outsourcing?* Obviously few buyers will tell the potential supplier what price to bid at, but the supplier needs to probe to check that there is some meeting of expectations. There is no point in going to the expense of preparing a bid for £5 million, when the buyer is expecting bids of less than half this amount. What can be explored more easily is whether the buyer has allocated a budget for its own expenses in managing the transformation process. A naïve buyer may believe that it will incur no costs and, if no budget is provided for the buyer's own activities, the project may fail.

- *Is the time scale realistic?* There are two aspects to this matter. It may be that no supplier could meet the time requirements, in which case it could be worth discussing this issue with the buyer in order to modify requirements. It could also be that this particular supplier is not in a position to move as quickly as the buyer would wish, although others could, in which case it would be better to decline to bid.

- *Is the buyer committed to outsourcing?* This is a question of identifying the decision-makers and influencers and of understanding the motivation of the key personnel.
- *How many firms are being invited to bid?* One management colleague of our acquaintance was invited to bid by a government agency for the development of some training materials. He told us that there were 11 organizations on the short list. If there are too many competitors bidding, it may not be worth continuing with the process.
- *What contract terms and conditions have been preset by the buyer?* Some buyers' procedures will be more bureaucratic than others. The British government, for example, has requirements that many suppliers feel make the whole bid process more expensive. In addition, the terms are said to make the suppliers accept an unfair proportion of the risks, even if the government itself caused the problem. You may recall that in the Passport Agency case a number of bids were rejected because they did not comply with all the required conditions. Some organizations are now declining to bid on these contracts.
- *Is the task something the supplier can do?* Even the largest and most capable of suppliers can sometimes be faced with a task that is beyond either its capability or its capacity. The factors to consider here will determine whether the supplier opts to continue or not (assuming that the buyer has not exercised its option to ask the firm not to bid). There are four aspects to consider.
  - *Does the scale and nature of the task match the available resources?* This question refers to the totality of the free

resources, including those obtained from alliances and outsourcing. The resources required may include more than industry, technical and managerial skills. Language capabilities and country knowledge may also be necessary.

— *Would it be possible to deliver solutions that matched the requirements?* This is a more subtle version of the above question. All the capabilities may be available, but the supplier may be uncomfortable with the measurements by which progress will be monitored, or the buyer's emphasis may be on aspects that the supplier finds unappealing for some reason. It may be that success is dependent on specific actions by the buyer that the supplier doubts will take place.

— *Is there likely to be compatibility with the client?* This may be unimportant if it is the factory canteen that is being outsourced, but vital if it is a project that requires both buyer and supplier to work as partners. If the cultures of the two organizations are very different, or if it is impossible to develop a partnership mentality with the buyer (rather than a master and servant arrangement), the chances of success may be much reduced. For the supplier there are two types of success, both of which are of equal importance. One is to have a satisfied client and the other is to operate within the project budget so that the work is profitable. Culture clashes can also affect relations with a buyer's employees who are expected to transfer to the supplier. If, for example, they come from the type of industrial relations culture described in the Timex Dundee case, it may be a disaster to employ them as a group.

— *What differentiation can the supplier offer?* Is this a project for which the supplier can offer a unique package, or an innovative solution that will add value to the client? Or is it effectively a situation in which the contract will be awarded partly on the buyer's feelings about the firm, but mainly on price? Clear differentiation may enable the supplier to obtain a better price and ideally should mean that the buyer benefits by obtaining more value than was expected.

Preparing the bid

There are four possible outcomes from the first two stages of the entry process: (1) the buyer may not ask the supplier to bid; (2) the supplier may decide not to bid; both parties may want to move to the next stage; (3) there may be some modification to the buyer's requirements; and (4) both parties may wish to proceed to a bid. The first stages are important to both parties because it may be the start of a relationship that both parties should see as something beyond the traditional view of a supplier. The relationship begins to be built through the pre-bid discussions and the rest of the bidding process. Whether it develops further depends on whether the bid is won, but even a losing bid may have impressed the buyer and lead to the chance of winning in a future buying opportunity.

For a large contract with many elements the process of bid preparations may involve a number of people and many hours of work. The work level involved may not always be realized by the buyer because only certain types of organization record how managers and professional people spend their time and are conscious of the cost of such personnel. Whereas the supplier is likely to be very aware of the costs of bidding, the buyer may not be.

The tasks of the supplier are not necessarily set out in the order they will appear in any proposal. We also take as given that the proposal will define the objectives of the contract and issues around these and will also demonstrate the competence of the supplier to handle these objectives. The supplier has to take account of following:

- All the components of the bid should be pulled together. This task involves assembling the team who will work on the project if the bid is successful and involving experts from each of the areas of activity in calculating labour requirements, costs and capital requirements.
- A critical path and/or other ways of interrelating schedules and tasks should be developed. In a simple project a Gantt chart may be adequate, but for anything more complex considerable analytical thought has to be applied. Not all skills may be needed at the same time, and labour requirements may vary with different phases of the work. The task needs to be tackled carefully because the overall costing and time phasing of the project budget may be critical for profitability as well as for planning the use of professional staff, some of whom will not be fully utilized on the contract. The buyer needs to see how the supplier will meet the required time scale and how to plan for any variation in the numbers of people who will be working on its premises. It should be clear how much time is needed for the transition stage before a normal state can be reached.
- The proposal should make very clear the aims of the contract, what precisely needs to be done and by when and the ways in which performance is measured.
- A risk assessment should be made so that the areas of vulnerability may be removed, if at all possible, or the consequences fully understood, if they cannot be removed.
- The factors for success will include many that are dependent on actions by the buyer. These actions need to be spelled out in some detail so that both parties are clear about them from

the outset and factor them into the critical path. Ideally, actions required by the buyer should be clearly defined in clauses in the contract for situations in which they are critical.

- Other success factors may hang on the performance of a third organization used by the buyer that is not a party to the contract. It is prudent to identify these factors and to pass the responsibility for compliance to the buyer.
- It is sensible to indicate how the contract, if won, will be managed, dealing particularly with the interface between the two organizations, regular discussion of performance, and early identification of problems. Provision for dealing with disputes should also be included, ideally giving a platform for dealing with problems before they become legalistic grievances.
- The financial part of the proposal should make it clear what the buyer will be charged, the timing of invoices, variations that are permitted because of volume changes, compensation for failure of the supplier to achieve the critical service targets, payment for any delays caused by the client and other relevant matters. Payment terms should be established. The deliverables should be clearly specified. Although at first sight it may appear to be in the supplier's interest to be as vague as possible, in fact this approach can lead to misunderstandings, disputes and eventually to a debased relationship with the buyer.
- Cancellation clauses should specify the compensation rights of each party in the event that a contract is terminated without just cause.
- It is also important that the terminology used in the contract is properly defined. Even simple words like 'day' can be interpreted in many different ways.
- Many of the requirements will be set out in the bid documents. In some cases the bid document may provide an outline contract into which the supplier has to fit its proposals.

Supplier Challenge 3 – Running the contract

If there are four bidders who go though to the final stages, there
will be three losers. It is important to lose gracefully, however disappointing the result may be. A pragmatic reason is that there may
be an opportunity to bid for other contracts in the organization at
a later date, so maintaining good relations may be in the supplier's
best interests. Even when this is not the case, a bidder who has been
impressive may well be recommended to other companies.

For the winner there is now the problem of running a complex
contract that will require a very different approach to that of the
traditional buyer and seller arrangement. The type of relationship
with the customer depends on what each party does once the contract is granted. For the supplier, the worst position is to be viewed
within the buyer organization as a traditional supplier, and for the
buyer it is equally damaging to take this view. With the critical and
strategic types of outsourcing, supplier and buyer have to develop
a relationship that is more akin to a partnership or alliance. If this
relationship breaks down, it may be very difficult for the full aims of
the contract to be achieved: instead of managing the relationship,
the buyer may try to administer it. This approach will only work
effectively when outsourcing peripheral activities such as security
or garden maintenance.

It takes two to build a working partnership relationship, but here
are some points for suppliers:

- Establish multi-level contact points. At the top there should be
  an accessible project manager who has regular formal and informal contact with the senior managers of the buyer. Support
  this with a periodic formal meeting at which appropriate level
  managers from both organizations meet to discuss progress, deal
  with issues, and anticipate problems. Below there should be clear

contact points at various points in the supplier organization so that issues can be dealt with at an operational level.

- Ensure that the contact people in the supplier organization who are working on the contract are properly empowered to take decisions and know the limits of their authority. What the buyer feels about the relationship is affected by what happens at all levels and not just by whether the senior people get on well.

- Be ready to change personnel if there are situations of personality clash. Such clashes will occur from time to time and buyer judgement will be affected by how quickly such issues are identified and dealt with. It is far better to transfer someone to another project before an irritation becomes a running sore than to try to defend a personal situation that has turned septic. The transferred individual should not be blamed unless he/she has a track record of such clashes.

- Ensure that all personnel who are working with the buyer understand fully the aims of the project and not just the technical aspects.

- Make sure that involved personnel really understand the buyer and its business at least as well as the buyer's own employees.

- Protect financial position, but do not become too legalistic when dealing with the buyer. There may well be problems and issues faced by the buyer for which it would be in no one's interest to refuse to take action because they were not covered by the contract. A partnership implies that both parties should try to help each other out of difficulties and there may be times when aspects of the contract should be modified, or concessions made to help the buyer to deal with a problem, such as a sudden dip in activity.

- Be proactive. First, try to anticipate and deal with issues early, when it is often less expensive to take action. Second, be innovative, suggest improvements and keep the buyer aware of new developments. Obviously, what can be done will depend on the nature of the outsourcing contract.

Case study: Driver and Vehicle Licensing Agency (DVLA), UK

A somewhat different perspective on the varying buyer expectations of a partnership rather than a more traditional approach to outsourcing is illustrated by the appointment of PWC Consulting, supported by Fujitsu Services, as the DVLA's IT and strategic business partner. The contract is worth $465.5 million over 10 years, and replaces the existing customer/supplier-style outsourcing arrangement with EDS that expired in December 2002. EDS had won the contract in 1993.[1] The DVLA press statement of 13 December 2002 included the following comment from Chief Executive Clive Bennet:

> This represents an exciting prospect for the Agency, which involves working with our PACT partner as an integrated team to deliver a programme of improved and innovative services to DVLA customers. Part of the focus will be on how we can harness and use cutting edge technology to make ideas like Electronic Vehicle Licensing a reality through a variety of different channels.
>
> It is also a unique opportunity for DVLA and PWC Consulting to become a centre of excellence and enterprise within Government.
>
> Significantly for the local community, this not only helps ensure the Agency's future as a major employer in the area but will also, through a new private sector employer established in Swansea, provide additional job opportunities.

[1] *Management Consultants' News Direct*, Issue 49, 23 September 2002.

Insight into how the partnering relationship is viewed by the DVLA is provided by the following extract from the business prospectus that was the basis of the contract. It is Crown copyright, reproduced under a general permission given to this document.

Appendix B to the DVLA Strategic Partnering Relationship Business Prospectus. January 2001

Purpose   This Annex provides potential suppliers with an insight into what DVLA means when it refers to a 'strategic partnering relationship' elsewhere in this Prospectus.

This Annex describes in overview what the partnering relationship means to DVLA, states DVLA corporate values and cites some example partnering principles.

Overview of Partnering Relationship   DVLA wishes to enter into a long-term strategic business partnering where both parties are working innovatively and flexibly to mutually agreed objectives and are prepared to share in the associated risks and rewards.

Partnering Mission   DVLA proposes the following as a mission statement for the partnering relationship:

'To enable the Agency to become the best in class amongst registration and licensing service providers on an international basis by implementing a programme of business change that provides modernised delivery channels for government services and exploits new business opportunities, whilst protecting the wider needs of the communities within which DVLA operates.'

DVLA's Values   The DVLA Executive Board has agreed to
a set of corporate values that they wish
to underpin the conduct of the Agency's
business and support the delivery of its
vision and mission. They are contained in
the acronym PRIDE and reflect the way in
which DVLA would wish to enter into a
strategic partnering relationship. The values are:

Partnership
Consider, treat and involve colleagues, customers and suppliers with respect regardless of status.

Responsibility
Clearly defined roles and responsibilities,
designed to provide added value and delivered to best ability to the benefit of internal
and external customers.

Integrity
Accountability for actions and an honest
and open approach to work.

Dedication
Commitment to service excellence and
to continuously seek ways of improving
the performance of the Agency. Colleagues
listen to and share views openly, con-
structively and respectfully.

Enjoyment
Work is designed to be enjoyable and ful-
filling.

Example Partnering Principles

DVLA recognises that it will need to work closely with its chosen partner to achieve its objectives. DVLA has, therefore, developed a number of example partnering principles that serve to define the nature of the relationship that DVLA wishes to develop with its chosen partner and which DVLA would expect to see emulated in return. Furthermore, DVLA is committed to partnership with the Trade Union at DVLA (Public and Commercial Services Union – PCS). The Agency's chosen partner will also be expected to build a partnering relationship with PCS.

Top Level Leadership

The partnering relationship will be championed at the top of both organisations. DVLA's Chief Executive will invest time and effort in ensuring that his commitment to the partnering relationship and his relationship with his counterpart in the partner organisation will be the role model for emulation throughout the organisations.

Top Level Interaction

The relationship will be managed from the top-level via meetings at peer level; Board to Board/CE to CE and involve participation between the parties at all levels e.g. the chosen partner, through consultation with DVLA, will be invited to attend certain meetings of the DVLA Executive Board. The ultimate purpose is to establish a relationship that enables a crisis to be handled maturely by both parties.

Open Dialogue

The dialogue between DVLA and its chosen partner will be open to prevent surprises and misconstructions arising for either party. DVLA will have no hidden agendas and will for example be prepared to discuss:

a. expectations about strategic direction, budgets, revenues and margins;
b. emerging problems before they become difficult to resolve;
c. key staff changes and the consequences for continuity of the partnering relationship.

Co-operation

The normal mode of working will be collaborative. DVLA is prepared to establish joint teams to address specific business issues. The chosen partner will be invited to work on joint business cases and input to business planning.

Mutual Respect

The partnering relationship will be built on mutual respect. DVLA does not intend to emphasise the power of formal authority. It will however engage in robust and constructive debate. DVLA will continue to do business without rancour regardless of the outcome.

Proactive

The partnering relationship will be managed using a proactive approach. DVLA will seek to ensure that forward thinking and innovative individuals are employed in managing the partnering relationship.

Constructive Questioning

There will be a focus on achieving agreed business outcomes, identifying benefits for both parties, finding solutions rather than finding obstructions.

Fairness

The parties will enter into a contract in the expectation that issues, problems, disputes, difficulties and unexpected developments will be resolved fairly so as not to bring undue advantage or disadvantage to either side. Fairness should reflect a reasonable and balanced view of the parties' obligations and commitment to each other within the context of the obligations under the contract.

The challenges for buyers

Much of what we have said about suppliers has its mirror image on the buyer side of arrangements. The DVLA case study makes a useful bridge between the two.

Whether an outsourcing decision will achieve its objectives and whether the appropriate relationship will be developed with the supplier begins before a supplier is approached. Unrealistic expectations, or a failure to understand the implications of the type of outsourcing arrangement sought, may mean that a workable relationship with the supplier can never be developed. As we saw in earlier chapters, there may be many good reasons why buyers seek particular types of outsourcing arrangements, but there are also some poor reasons.

The worst reason for making a decision to outsource is fad-following. Outsourcing has become fashionable and the height of fashion is to have a strategic relationship. Few buyers will believe that they are simply following a fad because rationalization takes place and numerous reasons for the decision can be identified. There is considerable evidence suggesting that managers adopt and discard strategies involving new tools and techniques with rather limited forethought.

Hilmer and Donaldson (1996) argue that overreliance on the validity of techniques is one of the five fads of modern management that tempts organizations along false trails. Although outsourcing is hardly a technique, their remarks are equally pertinent to methods and processes. Techniques and tools can be of immense benefit, provided they are appropriate for the situation and are correctly applied. However, they are not a replacement for sound management:

Techniques for all. As problems arise, find the appropriate solution technique and apply it quickly . . . the good manager need not go back to first principles or hard thinking, but instead should pick up and religiously implement the 'right' technique or program. This is 'instant coffee' management – 'just open the can and add water – no work required'. (Hilmer and Donaldson, 1996)

They argue that the easy acceptance of the latest technique has much to do with the persuasive powers of many practitioners and writers:

> The case is put so simply, forcefully and fashionably that any other view sounds untenable, or even politically incorrect. (Hilmer and Donaldson, 1996)

Buyer Challenge 1 – The pre-bid phase

Before even developing a short list of suppliers, the buyer should develop a business case.

The first step is to define what is being sought and why. *Is the goal primarily cost savings, transfer of risks, avoiding a capital expenditure, solving a difficulty in obtaining enough employees in an area of scarce skills, gaining better access to the technology in a fast-developing field, obtaining tighter management focus on the critical issues, tying in to new sources of innovation, or something else?*

It is sensible to define these matters because, without this clarification, it is impossible to evaluate the decision to outsource, or to ensure that the right suppliers are identified. Although the DVLA case study does not include the full business case, it is clear that the organization has not only defined what it wants from a supplier, but also has given considerable thought to what the organization has to do to make the relationship work.

The other part of the equation is to properly understanding internal costs and the implications of the service or component targeted for outsourcing. It is sensible when the main driver is cost reduction to assess the improvements that could be obtained through internal actions. This analysis has to take a long-term view and great care should be taken to understand the basis of the cost analysis

and to fully understand any business processes that might be targets. This information is needed even when there are other reasons
besides cost reduction because it provides a baseline to help assess
the value to the firm of bids from suppliers.

An invitation-to-bid document should be prepared. This document should contain the key information on the organization that
any supplier would need to make a bid as well as clear details about
minimum expectations on performance standards. Common sense
indicates when it may be commercially damaging to give out too
much information, lest it create a self-fulfilling prophecy. It may be
sensible to give a statement that the buyer is seeking a significant reduction of costs, but foolish to state the exact percentage. It may be
reasonable to provide volume figures for a component with details
of seasonal variations, but it may not be clever to state the current
cost of production.

A common complaint is that such documents from government
departments are too complex, making the bid process very expensive. Overcomplexity should be avoided, but there is a need to give
enough information, including what will become key clauses in the
contract, to enable suppliers to respond.

Buyer Challenge 2 – Identifying
the key suppliers

Just as the supplier would not want to bid for business with an organization that was halfway into insolvency, so the buyer does not
want a supplier who lacks the resources to provide long-term sustainability. Also important is an overview of the competence and
track record of the organization. All of this intelligence gathering
can be done by desk research, informal discussion and discreet enquiries. Furthermore, some of the suppliers are likely already known
to the buyer.

The selection process can be handled in a variety of ways, and the private sector can dispense with a competitive bid if it wishes. Public sector organizations are forced to take competitive bids from anyone who wishes to do so, hence some of the dissatisfaction mentioned elsewhere in this book among certain suppliers bidding for British government outsourcing contracts. A pre-qualification process can save everyone a great deal of work by eliminating suppliers who clearly cannot match the needs of the assignment in terms of capacity, experience, financial resources, competence, or culture. If you are looking to establish a strategic relationship, it may be unwise to consider a supplier whose only experience is with traditional supplier/buyer relationships.

For large contracts that will stretch over a number of years, there is clear sense in selecting a short list of suppliers who will be invited to make a formal bid. The relationship with the supplier who is eventually chosen will begin here. The quality of the proposal, in terms of the way the supplier interprets what the buyer wants and responds to it, and the innovation shown is important. The bid process also provides opportunities for the buyer and supplier to explore the issues together and to see how personal chemistry develops between managers in the two organizations.

Buyer Challenge 3 – Awarding the contract

Eventually there is only one winner. Of course, the winner will be chosen based on a mix of criteria, including costs. The DVLA had a very clear idea of some of the mechanisms that it would need to establish in order to make its view of strategic partnership work. However, it is probable that the winning supplier built on this foundation, showing its mirror actions, but also providing additional substance and making suggestions of its own. Asking for such ideas may be an early step in building the relationship and it immediately takes the relationship beyond the traditional outsourcing arrangement.

Buyer Challenge 4 – Running the contract

What we said under a similar heading when considering suppliers contains much that is valid for the buyer, and that advice will not be repeated here. Although in many situations the supplier will have more experience of outsourcing relationships than the buyer, it is the buyer who has to take a leadership role. The supplier can take steps that frustrate any attempt at partnership, but it is the buyer whose actions and attitudes at all levels will determine the sustainability of the relationship.

Suppliers expect to be held to the quality, performance and service levels agreed at the outset, although the style of the reviews and discussions are important as already mentioned. Sometimes one or other of the parties has to establish a way of monitoring performance. The Passport Agency case discussed in an earlier chapter overlooked one key element in performance measurement, which until it was corrected meant that incorrect judgements were being made.

Forgetting to monitor is no way to achieve a meaningful relationship. As Jennings (2002) states:

> A survey of UK private and public sector organisations by Shreeveport Management Consultancy (1997) concluded that little more than half of the surveyed companies measured the performance of outsourced services to ensure that claimed benefits were achieved.

Summary

In this chapter we have looked at the various issues that should concern a supplier of outsourced services and then flipped the coin to look at the various issues that should concern the buyer of outsourced services. We illustrate some of the potential pitfalls involved in buyer/supplier relationships and discuss various ways of overcoming the problems through effective management of relationships at each step of the supplying and the buying processes.

References

Doig, S. J., Ritter, R. C., Speckhals, K. and Woolson, D. 2001. Has outsourcing gone too far? *McKinsey Quarterly*, No. 4.

Hilmer, F. and Donaldson, L. 1996. The trivialisation of management, *McKinsey Quarterly*, No. 4.

Hodson, N. 2002. Outsourcing from the supplier perspective. *Journal of Professional HRM*, January, Issue 26.

Hussey, D. 1999. Some thoughts on acquisition and merger, *Strategic Change*, January, Vol. 8, No. 1, pp. 51–60.

Hussey, D. 2002. *Business driven HRM*, 2nd edition, John Wiley & Sons Ltd, Chichester.

Jennings, D. 2002. Outsourcing: motives and policy, *Journal of Professional HRM*, January.

KPMG, 2001. *World class transactions: Insights into creating shareholder value*, KPMG, London.

Martin, G. and Dowling, M. 1995. Managing change, Human Resource Management and Timex, *Journal of Strategic Change*, March–April, Vol. 4, No. 2.

Ozanne, M. 2000. *Barometer of global outsourcing*, Dun & Bradstreet.

Shreeveport Management Consultancy 1997. Outsourcing: the real story, *Financial Times*, 10 December.

Pricing solutions and managing risks

5

Introduction

In this chapter we look at the value of strategic pricing and the fundamental pricing concepts that affect the pricing of solutions for outsourcing and facilities management contracts. The arguments in favour of bundling in pricing involving 'packaged deals' and unbundling options involving pricing of individual components are discussed, as are the pricing implications of employing distributors. A range of price administration issues is reviewed and a short assessment of the risks associated with pricing solutions for buyers and suppliers is provided. The chapter concludes with suggestions for managing the uncertainties associated with pricing solutions and a short series of recommendations on the management of pricing taking into account both profits and risks.

The value of strategic pricing

Both buyers and suppliers have concerns about pricing and risks in any business relationship.

The statement is true for all aspects of commerce, of course, but it is particularly an issue in outsourcing and facility management contracts. In the development and negotiation of such contracts, this is the Gordian knot that must be resolved to the satisfaction of all parties to a relationship for an optimal outcome.

Although the purchasing literature contains ample discussions on how such contracts or service level agreements (SLAs) should be structured (e.g., Aubert *et al.*, 2002), little discussion has been devoted to the perspective of vendors. Although few marketing decisions have the apparent simplicity of the pricing decision, no other aspects of marketing have greater significance for commercial success and profitability over the lifespan of a customer–vendor relationship. However, our experience suggests that the pricing decision is one of the most complex decisions facing the marketer, yet very few managers think strategically about the company's pricing policies. Nagle and Holden (2002) have argued that in most companies the difference between price setting and strategic pricing involves the difference between reacting to market conditions and proactively managing them. Strategic pricing, it is argued, involves coordination of interrelated marketing, competitive factors, and financial decisions as well as balancing the inherent risks of selling solutions for profitable outcomes. However, the experience of many of the companies in our outsourcing research project was that apparently attractive and profitable possibilities in the solution market often turned out to be loss-making or marginally profitable when the endeavour was viewed over time and evaluated from an activity-based costing perspective.

Fundamental pricing concepts

In the general marketing literature, there are three dominant types of pricing decisions:

- Cost-plus pricing
- Competitor or benchmark pricing
- Value pricing.

We will elaborate on the three generic pricing strategies below.

The *cost-plus pricing* method has historically been the most common pricing procedure in industrial markets as well as among many outsourcing firms. This method builds on an accounting picture of the allocated costs of components and activities involved in creating an offering, plus a prudent yield allowing the company a fair return for its efforts. Although it seems to be a simple guide to a profitable way of achieving satisfactory results, it often creates an illusion because of difficulties in determining an offering's actual costs before establishing the price. Because of the difficulties in estimating the true costs of the offering, companies often engage in odd assumptions and rules of thumb. For example, when a large customer is lost, the fixed overhead of the company is allocated to other offerings, causing the unit cost, and consequently the price, to increase thereby jeopardizing other customer relationships as a result of increased prices. Because the competitive context is not taken into account, it can be argued that cost-plus pricing generally leads to overpricing when the seller is in a weak market position and underpricing when in a strong market; from a competitive viewpoint, the opposite often would be more strategically correct.

The *benchmark pricing* method suggests that the firm sets prices in accordance with what it perceives is the 'market price' as established by other firms. This approach is often exercised by smaller players in a dynamic industry in which there appears to be little possibility of creating variation in the offer and influencing customers' buying behaviour using other parameters than competitive pricing. Savants refer to this as 'letting the tail wag the dog' (Nagle and Holden, 2002, p. 7). The economic literature describes this situation as a company being a price taker, and the only way to increase market share is through aggressive pricing. Yet, one can question whether a market share goal is the right, or even the relevant, objective.

Value pricing is sometimes labelled 'customer-driven pricing'. This method is gaining in importance as companies increasingly acknowledge the erroneous biases of cost-based pricing, its bias to decision-making and the impact on profitability. The argument of taking pricing decisions away from the accounting department and placing them in the hands of product/marketing management emphasizes the efforts to deliver value to customers. Thus, the pricing should reflect the contribution that a solution delivers to the customer, and should echo the positioning of the marketing mix. Not only is there an attempt to deliver a solution that satisfies the customer by reflecting the customer's preferences in the bundle of goods and services delivered, but also there is an attempt to produce the desired profitability by identifying value opportunities in the marketplace (Hayes *et al.*, 1995).

In practice, marketing managers often have a difficult time determining customers' perceptions of the value of a given product, despite the use of relatively sophisticated marketing research techniques, such as conjoint analysis (Green and Rao, 1971). It is very difficult to 'get inside' the customers' activity cycles in order to understand how the proposed solution will affect their cost structures, their ability to satisfy clients and competitiveness, their speed of delivery and their profitability. The difficulty lies in the model building that needs to take place and the assumptions that must be made during this process. The model building requires an intimate understanding of each customer's business and the value of the trade-offs being made. Even if it is possible to gain access to staff in customers' organizations, the challenge is to build a uniform picture of their values and their cost data, which will vary with the perspectives of different participants and influencers in the buying decision and also with time as the power or importance of different perspectives changes. Furthermore, even if it is possible to develop a workable model to assess the value derived by the customer from using a particular bundle of goods and services, it is still necessary to take into account competitive offers and substitutes, including in-house production.

On this basis we argue that pricing has more impact than any other marketing decision. Pricing has a highly significant impact on revenues, and thus on profits, often in unexpected ways. Because the price a customer will pay is affected by the customer's perception of the value of the product or service, all other marketing decisions come together in the pricing decision. In other words, the price at which the firm elects to offer its solutions and services should represent the firm's belief about their value to a particular target market. Therefore, it should take into account all the benefits the customer may receive, including both tangible and intangible aspects of the product offering, its availability, its added value arising from sales force performance and, most importantly, its competitive positioning relative to substitute products and services.

Pricing the bundle of goods and services

In the market for outsourcing, price bundling is the most common approach across many sectors ranging from cleaning services to outsourcing IT functions and manufacturing facilities management, although the rationale may not always be clearly articulated. Price bundling is highly effective because the combined bundle has a particular integrated value in the eyes of the customer that often is higher than if each of the components of the offer were priced individually. Take the example of the sale of an integrated IT systems solution. A systems integration project can roughly be divided into the following generic core elements:

- Definition of the engineering or business problem
- Conceptualization of a technical or business solution
- Specification of a proposal/work plan to solve the problem and implement the solution
- Definition of the project and who is going to do the actual work
- Evaluation of and choice among alternative proposals

- Implementation of project
- Evaluation of project.

When firms such as IBM or other solution providers engage in the business for integrated IT solutions the first four elements will often be an integral part of the request for proposal (RFP) and will often be carried out at no cost to the customer under the assumption that the project subsequently will pay for the work performed. Yet, a survey of customers of integrated IT solutions suggests that a large part of the perceived value in the eyes of customers actually rests on the ability of the vendor to articulate the correct problem, develop a compelling concept, detail a proposal and pull a competent team together. The perceived value to the customer of these four elements was reported informally again and again in customer surveys as from 40% to 45% of the overall value of IT solution. However, often these steps are not being invoiced because they are seen as part of the selling process.

The 'bundling versus unbundling' decisions for an offer have both advantages and disadvantages. In many instances it may be advantageous for the supplier to bundle parts of the offering, either to offer a package combination at a lower price than if service components were offered separately, or to tie the sale of components with little competitive advantage to those with significant advantage. The decision to bundle or unbundle is influenced by a number of factors. In some instances, customers may pressure the supplier to unbundle the package because they may not wish to purchase all the solution components in the bundle, as might be the case with training or special application assistance. In other instances, tying the sale of a service component with great competitive advantage to one with little advantage may be viewed negatively, not only by customers but also by regulatory authorities. The latter was true in the case of IBM when it was required by the US Department of Justice to unbundle the sale of mainframe computers and software.

Pricing when distributors are involved

If the firm sells the offer directly to its customers, it then has complete control over the price at which it offers its services. When distributors, or other intermediaries, such as value-adding partners, are involved, the price at which these middlemen offer the solution must be taken into account in the price determination process. There are two key questions, the first of which is: What is the distributor's margin? The distributor's margin should reflect the functions performed by the distributor. In most cases, a normal margin for a particular class of product sold to a particular industry will have evolved over time, reflecting industry experience and competitive practices. In the American machine tool industry, for instance, margins for full service distributors offering service contracts may range from 7.5% to 15%, depending on the service offering.

The second, and equally important, question is: To what extent can the vendor control the price at which the distributor offers the product or service? In most industrialized countries, vertical price fixing (i.e., a specific agreement between manufacturer and distributor as to the price to be charged) is illegal. In theory, distributors are free to set prices at whatever level they choose, regardless of the normal margin. In practice, however, manufacturers can exert considerable influence over the distributor's price. In particular, it is usually legal for a manufacturer to indicate, if in fact it so desires, that it expects its distributors to adhere to its suggested user prices. Distributors who do not do so may be terminated.

Price administration

The administration of the price structure also poses a challenge when viewed over time. Three issues deserve consideration – the issue of list versus net pricing, the issue of discounts and the issue of transaction pricing.

For a number of reasons, vendors may elect to publish a schedule of prices in list and discount form rather than as net prices. Where distributors are involved, the list prices may indicate suggested user prices to be charged by distributors. Use of list prices, subject to some level of discount, facilitates price changes that can be implemented simply by changing the discount rather than by revising prices on an item-by-item basis. Use of list prices also provides a basis for offering quantity discounts, a frequent business marketing practice. Finally, anecdotal evidence indicates that at least some purchasing agents prefer a list and discount price approach because they can report the discount as a saving achieved through aggressive purchasing practice.

Discounts are used in a number of additional ways. Functional discounts to distributors reflect the level of service provided by a distributor, or the manufacturer's cost to serve a particular market. A limited service distributor in a particular industry, providing only stocking and sales, might receive a discount of 20%, whereas a full service distributor providing stocking, sales and service might receive a larger discount of 23–25% or, as frequently expressed, 20 and 5. Typically strategic accounts may receive additional discounts, perhaps another 5–15%, reflecting both functions performed and the amount of business, or the amount expended by the client on project-specific investments.

In the price discussion, a number of special pricing issues can arise. Examples of such issues include those associated with pricing across country borders when, for example, cost levels may vary, currencies may fluctuate and tax and depreciation rules may differ.

A unique aspect of some outsourcing markets, such as sales to public institutions, and also of many business deals is the frequent use of sealed bidding, for which buyers require formal quotations or bids with no opportunity for subsequent negotiation. Some buyers will specify so completely the required outsourcing project that the purchase decision can be made on the basis of price alone. More frequently, the decision is made on the basis of the 'lowest and best bid', suggesting that some service attributes may be evaluated, either adding to or subtracting from the bid price. In the case of public procurement, the norm is for the bids to be publicly opened, affording bidders the opportunity to determine all aspects of competitive offerings. In the case of private procurement practices vary, but the norm is to reveal very little regarding competitive offerings.

In either case, price determination is challenging. A number of models have been proposed to assist in price determination, generally built around an expected value approach based on the following formula:

$$E(X) = P(X)Z(X)$$

where X = the bid price, $Z(X)$ = the profit at the bid price, $P(X)$ = the probability of an award at this price, and $E(X)$ = the expected profit of a bid. The assumption is that the price bid should be the one with the highest expected profit.

Empirical evidence indicates that such models are extremely limited in their application. In our observations of the practices of general contractors in the construction industry, for which sealed bidding is the norm, less than 10% of the respondents reported use of a statistical bidding model, payoff table, or probability model in preparing the bid. This limited use reflects a number of problems in using such a model. Probability estimates are highly subjective, particularly in the absence of a long pattern of similar awards on which to base them. A number of other objectives beyond profit may influence the bid price, such as the prospect of follow-on work, maintaining a stable workforce, size of the backlog, and so forth. Still further, the prices bid on one transaction may influence prices on future transactions, and bidders may use a sealed bid, particularly if publicly opened, as a way to communicate future pricing intentions.

Given this complexity, the final determination of the price to be bid or quoted will depend heavily on the experience and intuition of the manager. In appropriate circumstances, however, expected value models can assist this decision-making process.

A discussion on pricing would not be complete without discussing the challenges of *price fixing*. Stable prices in oligopolistic markets are not necessarily a sign of price fixing. Price stability vanishes in the face of profit pressures arising from low demand and from aggressive moves to obtain orders by competitors that may drive prices below full costs. In many industries, such aggressive pricing has led to price wars, motivating managers to seek agreement with competitors on price levels, or look for other ways to eliminate price competition. In the United States such agreements violate the Sherman Antitrust Law. In the European Union, they violate Article 85 of the Treaty of Rome (the treaty that first established the European Economic Community). Additionally, most industrialized countries similarly prohibit such agreements, particularly those that prevent, restrict, or distort competition. In Germany, for instance, there is extensive anti-cartel legislation, administered by the Federal Cartels Office, and in the United Kingdom the Competition Act of 1980 gives powers to the Director General of Fair Trading to investigate anticompetitive practices, including price fixing.

There is a fine line between the kind of stability suggested by the role of a price leader, generally followed by others in the industry, and price fixing. In the United States the Department of Justice has long been concerned with 'conscious parallelism', a concept holding that violation of the Sherman Act does not necessarily require a specific agreement to fix prices but can occur when competitors, simply by virtue of long association, have reached some common understandings about pricing that have the same effect on industry prices as overt collusion. As a result, the Department of Justice has frequently sought, and obtained, agreement on the part of firms to discontinue practices that facilitate conscious parallelism, such as price changes that all competitors in the industry make in a short period of time and in the same amounts. Announcements of aluminium price changes in the business press, for instance, were deemed to have been targeted more at competitors than at customers. The Department of Justice successfully obtained an agreement from major producers to discontinue the practice. Other actions have been more stringent. In one industry the major competitors were required to completely discontinue the use of published prices and to fully revise the basis on which prices had previously been calculated in order to ensure that quoted prices were arrived at independently.

The concern about price fixing, and the degree to which various activities may be illegal, varies around the world. In Switzerland, for instance, some forms of price agreements are still legal. Nevertheless, it behooves business marketers to fully understand and abide by provisions of antitrust legislation or competition policy.

Understanding the risks to suppliers and buyers

There are three types of costs to be considered both for buyers and sellers in an outsourcing arrangement: the cost of the solution to be offered, the cost of bargaining (e.g., negotiating contract details, negotiating contract changes in the post-contract stage when unforeseen circumstances arise, direct and indirect costs of performance monitoring relative to the agreed terms) and the cost of disagreement arising when the resolution mechanisms of the negotiated agreement are not followed by either party (Vining and Globerman, 1999).

The costs of bargaining arise as an issue when both parties are acting on the basis of self-interest, but in *good* faith according to Williamson (1985). These incremental costs of outsourcing are of relevance both to the buyer and the seller. Buyers need to consider these costs because the alternative is often to perform the activity internally (although the internal costs of salaries and transfer prices also can create complications). For sellers, these transaction costs are partly included in the general sales and administrative costs, but for firms just starting out to supply outsourcing services, such costs are often vastly underestimated and the risks are poorly understood.

Another important cost is derived from so-called *opportunistic behaviour* by which a company attempts to sway the agreement in its favour, but in *bad* faith as in the case of concealing information that might affect an outsourcing project negatively or positively. Since this type of behaviour is more likely to take place in outsourcing arrangements than between internal units performing the same activity, this type of cost has implications for both buyers and sellers. It should also be noted that such opportunistic behaviour is likely to take place both before and after the contract has been signed.

Similar costs are imposed on both parties when one party has relevant information that the other party does not possess. This unevenness in the availability of information has been entitled *information asymmetry*. The high complexity in most outsourcing projects suggests that the seller has unique competencies within the scope of the activity itself and the buyer's unique competencies focus on the complexities of the project context, hence the high likelihood of information asymmetry. The existence of information asymmetry leaves ample room for opportunistic behaviour, both in the pre-contract stage and also after the deal has been struck.

The above costs and the associated uncertainties surrounding the transactions make it difficult for both buyers who are anxious to get the desired products and sellers who are anxious to meet the quality of delivery within a cost tolerance.

Mechanisms for bridging uncertainties

One of the most common approaches for alleviating uncertainties about future costs is *indexed pricing*. Indexing the price, often in conjunction with the consumer price index, maintains relative value over the life of the agreement. It involves paying by the volume, cost drivers and market price. If measures to reduce costs are integrated with the indexed prices, there can be benefits for both the buyer and the seller. This type of pricing structure drives a continually lower cost solution partnership.

Performance-based pricing is another pricing model that includes conformance to requirements, availability, timeliness and continuous improvement. It represents an effort to more closely tie pricing to the delivery of valuable products and services and it also introduces more variability in pricing. Furthermore, pricing is more closely related to the value of the input. It is an inherently more sophisticated pricing structure requiring more thought and oversight to administer, but it still represents a front-end performance measurement as in the case of quality of service and speed of delivery.

Finally, customers and vendors in highly complex outsourcing relationships are starting to use *pricing models based on shared risks and rewards* as a major step toward linking compensation to end-user or back-end performance. This approach ensures that the connection to end-user goals is stronger. Such contracts often involve incentives such as gain sharing, value engineering, savings-based pricing, and revenue-based pricing. For example, when IBM and Mercedes-Benz formed an agreement at the car manufacturer's Alabama plant, not only were the incentives tied to IT-related activities, but they were also linked to meeting the plant's production quota. This reward structure made IBM part of the Mercedes team. For firms that are leaders in the industry or early adopters, there is a tremendous opportunity to strike these kinds of pricing deals because providers recognize that their customers' successes are also theirs.

Summary

Pricing solutions and managing risks for the delivery of outsourcing and also facilities management contracts have been the focus of this chapter. In conclusion, a few key points should be emphasized.

First, pricing methods and their use must be given serious attention by any seller, and in the outsourcing business this is particularly the case.

Second, value-based pricing must be the preferred approach, not only because it is likely to yield the highest profits but also because it forces the firm to think of the solution from the perspective of the client and the client's problems. These implications of value-based pricing are not negative for buyers because it is not the seller's profit which is the issue, but the costs to the customer.

Third, sellers may gain advantages from bundling activities because this approach can create greater cost efficiency, lower transaction costs and better protection of proprietary knowledge resulting in tighter customer lock-in. However, customers may attempt to get sellers to unbundle offerings when their own familiarity with the activities is high, or when the pricing of competitive offerings is very transparent.

Fourth, when distributors or intermediaries are involved, the challenge is always to determine the sharing of margins, activities and risks. When dis-intermediation takes place, the distributors disappear, but not their function.

Fifth, when firms are operating across different markets and borders, the price administration becomes complex, particularly when multinational clients are being served.

Sixth, thorough analysis of the risks must be included in the price determination, and also the ways in which these risks change over time. Here, there is a need for both buyers and sellers to collaborate in order to create durable long-term relationships.

References

Aubert, B., Houde, J. F., Patry, M. and Rivard, S. 2002. Characteristics of IT outsourcing contracts, Proceedings of the 36th Hawaii International Conference on System Sciences.

Green, P. E. and Rao, V. R. 1971. Conjoint measurement of quantifying judgmental data, *Journal of Marketing Research,* Vol. 8, No. 3, pp. 355–363.

Hayes, H. M., Jenster, P. V. and Aaby, N.-E. 1995. *Business marketing – A global perspective,* Irwin, Chicago.

Nagle, T. T. and Holden, R. K. 2002. *The strategy and tactics of pricing – A guide to profitable decision making*, 3rd edition, Pearson Higher Education, New Jersey.

Vining, A. and Globerman, S. 1999. A conceptual framework for understanding the outsourcing decision, Working Paper.

Williamson, O., 1985. *The economic institution of capitalism*, The Free Press, New York.

'Transitioning' human resources

6

Introduction

In this chapter[1] we look at the ways in which the management of human resources can play a critical role in the new relationships underlying the successful sale and marketing of total facilities management. We present an approach developed by an experienced international facilities manager to deal systematically with the relevant HR issues. In the ongoing debate regarding the use of outsourcing as a strategic management tool we take the position that placing a higher priority on 'people issues' is important for successful outsourcing, especially for total solutions provision.

Setting the scene

In January 2004 Nokia and IBM announced a major outsourcing agreement by which IBM took over management of PCs for 57 000 Nokia employees in 57 countries. The deal was worth about DKK 1.5 billion. In that process IBM assumed responsibility for employing some 430 Nokia employees (Breinstrup, 2004).

Despite the challenges associated with the transfer of a sizable number of personnel and the associated risks, discussions with

[1] This chapter builds on Jenster, P. V. and Pedersen, H. S. 1999. Deal maker or deal breaker: Human resources issues in successful outsourcing projects, *Journal of Strategic Change*, August, Vol. 8, pp. 263–268.

executives involved in large outsourcing contracts confirm that rarely are human resource issues put very high on the list of priority issues. Issues such as core competencies, strategy, efficiency and synergies are much higher priorities. Yet human resource issues are often pivotal to the success of outsourcing agreements. In the words of one HR executive with considerable experience in the management of outsourcing agreements at IBM Denmark, an organization that was a pioneer in providing total facilities management beginning in the early 1980s:

> A facilities management contract may fail or succeed; it largely depends on how the employee transfer is managed.[2]

Is it overly bold to assert that success or failure of a facilities management endeavour hinges to such a great extent on how the HR issues are managed? If this company's experience is indicative, and we believe that it is, the 'people issues' surrounding facilities management need to be given much higher priority than has previously been the case. Generally speaking, HR personnel do not become involved until after the agreement on facilities management is already in place. In our view human resource issues represent a very important – and often overlooked – element in the current debate on outsourcing. We argue that human resources issues will have to be given high priority in the sale and marketing of outsourcing and facilities management contracts in order to ensure operational success for the buying organization and financial success for the supplying firm.

In the large study on outsourcing conducted with companies in Denmark, the findings from the interviews suggest that the 'softer issues' in facilities management arrangements often are left unattended until after the contract has been signed. Such practices have proven to be both costly and detrimental to the success of

---

[2] We gratefully acknowledge the contribution of Ms Lisbeth Hald, former HR Executive with IBM Denmark, for her insight on total facilities management agreements.

outsourcing strategies. This finding suggests a new role for HR personnel in the selling organization involving the following tasks:

- To be on the marketing and sales team so that the sales document is comprehensive, including attention to legal and social dimensions of the transfer arrangements.
- To prepare the groundwork for the transfer of employees, e.g., communication with the employees and organizational preparations for the transfers.
- To engage in the entire process from the initial planning to the integration of new employees.
- To work inside the buying organization (the potential client) earlier in order to anticipate pitfalls and smooth the process of employee transfer.
- To provide stewardship of the transfer process so that the transferred employees are successfully integrated into the selling organization and their capabilities effectively utilized.

When a certain activity, previously undertaken by in-house employees, is transferred to the control of an outside company, these employees may continue to perform the same activity despite the fact that they are no longer employees of the company in which they physically carry out their work. This definition of *employee transfer* specifies that these employees have been 'transferred' to the company selling the facilities management services to the company outsourcing the activity (the buyer or client). Relationships between the *selling company* (e.g., IBM Denmark) and the *buying company* (client) are illustrated in Figure 6.1. The research findings from the large Danish outsourcing study mentioned above suggest that much outsourcing of IT departments is motivated by a critical shortage of competent personnel in the IT sector.

When undertaking facilities management contracts, companies are not only required to deliver a product and/or service on specific terms and conditions including criteria of satisfaction, but also

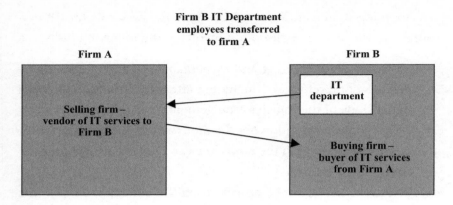

Figure 6.1 – Employee transfer under total facilities management outsourcing agreements.

are required in many cases to take managerial responsibility for employees at the client's premises – and very often these are former employees of the client. In light of this responsibility, companies engaged in facilities management need to ensure that their facilities management agreements:

- Define and operationalize the client's criteria of satisfaction for successful transfer of its former employees to the selling firm.
- Develop a strategy for managing the human resource issues of the transferred employees.

The fundamentals

The way a company deals with the transfer of employees basically reflects how it sees and understands human behaviour. For example, a company selling facilities management solutions wants to convince employees working at the client company that their transfer to the selling company is advantageous to them. Many different approaches could be taken. In the case of one company, the international facilities manager in question previously made the mistake of heavily overemphasizing the professional advantages that the employees stood to gain when they joined the company, e.g., career growth, promotion potential and educational opportunities, and severely underplayed the importance of the basic conditions of employment, e.g., salary, pensions and benefits. These basic conditions of employment were of vital interest and concern to the transferred employees. The emphasis placed by the organization in question on career advances as the most important advantage of being 'transferred' to its fold revealed the existence of a strong belief or assumption in the facilities management company that people are primarily guided and motivated by professional motives. In fact, *many different forces motivate people.*

One way to conceptualize human motivators is the familiar – and much cited – hierarchy of needs, developed by the American psychologist Abraham Maslow (1943; Vroom and Deci, 1970; Burnes, 1992). He was in fact one of the first to classify various types of human needs. Maslow's work, although not designed specifically for organizational analysis but rather for life in general, has been widely accepted by HR specialists and has had an enormous impact on job design and research (Burnes, 1992). Maslow's categories may be translated into a more HR-oriented management vocabulary. The five levels in Maslow's hierarchy of needs and the corresponding job-related translations are shown in Figure 6.2.

Maslow's hierarchy of needs, despite its simplicity, can be a useful tool when planning the transfer of employees. It should be remembered that it is just as serious to neglect the lower level, more basic needs as to ignore the higher level esteem and self-actualization needs of employees.

Maslow's hierarchy of human needs[1]	Job-related hierarchy of human needs[2]
Physiological needs – Need to address hunger, thirst, sleep, etc., and only when these basic needs have been satisfied will other needs emerge	Conditions of employment needs – Need for salary, pension, benefits, work hours, transport
Safety needs – Need for security and protection against danger	Job security needs – Need for stability, protection against arbitrary dismissal
Social needs – Need for feeling of belonging, for gaining love and affection	Need for social interaction with colleagues – Need for belonging to a company and/or a group
Esteem needs – Need for personal respect	Need for attention from management – Need for respect for professional achievements
Self-actualization needs – Need to be able to achieve one's full potential	Need for professional and personal development – Need for challenges, continuous learning and upgrading of competencies and career advances

[1] Maslow (1943).

[2] Adapted from conversations with Ms Lisbeth Hald, former HR Executive with IBM Denmark.

Figure 6.2 – Maslow's hierarchy and HR implications for employee transfers in facilities management contracts.

Strategies for employee transfer

The previous section presented a more theoretical view of human motivators and needs. It is a helpful tool for understanding how and why people behave and react in the way that they do. But what are the implications for the actual planning and implementation of the transfer of employees? The four-phase model outlined below provides some useful guidelines that we see as valuable for managers. This model is based on the systematic approach to facilities management agreements that was developed by IBM Denmark over the years since its pioneering efforts in the area of facilities management in the early 1980s.

Four-phase planning and implementation model for employee transfer:

- Phase 1 – Preparation and consulting
- Phase 2 – Communication
- Phase 3 – Recruitment
- Phase 4 – Orientation and development

Phase 1 – Preparation and consulting

The first phase consists of planning and counselling. This process starts before any contract has been concluded. In general, it is the selling company that consults with the buying company (client) to lay the groundwork for the transfer of its employees. This process is designed to ensure that the buying company is aware and equipped to deal with all of the necessary activities to ensure successful transfer.

The following activities are central in this phase:

- Investigate legal aspects and issues, e.g., labour rights, especially for public sector employees.
- Develop a communication plan, e.g., who will communicate, when will communication take place and how will communication be designed.
- Define conditions of employment, e.g., the conditions of employment in the supplying firm and whether they match or differ from those of the client.

- Establish conditions of employment, e.g., procedures for guiding the hiring process.
- Determine the appropriate organizational structure for the new employees.

The preparation phase often takes place concurrently with the selling phase when the companies are considering whether, and how, to enter into a facilities management contract. The experience at IBM Denmark strongly suggests the merit of HR personnel in the potential facilities management company taking an active part in the actual development of the sales document. In fact, the selling company (IBM Denmark) established an entire facilities management 'sales and transition team' including the lead salesperson, HR, personnel, an account manager, a transition manager to handle technical aspects and the project manager. The duration of the first phase depends on the number of employees affected by the contract. Before the companies proceed to the second phase, a letter of intent should be drafted.

Phase 2 – Communication

As can be imagined, many people and their interests will be affected by the process of transferring a certain activity previously undertaken by in-house employees to an outside company. The communication of how the transfer will affect the interests of these persons, the second phase, is particularly critical to the success of the facilities management contract. Now the communication activities, which were planned in the preceding phase, will be put into effect. If the contract is to succeed, then it is crucial that the (potential) supplier have completed Phase 1 – Preparation and consulting before the employees are informed of the outsourcing arrangement. This 'inside presence' is established during the preparation and consulting phase while the actual sales process is being concluded.

In order to design an effective internal communications strategy, it is necessary that the supplier have a thorough understanding of the communication needs and organizational structure of the supplier. The specific communications phase targets are:

- The employees directly affected by the facilities management contract
- The client/buying organization
- The selling company/supplier organizations
- External communication personnel who have responsibility for press releases and other communication activities.

Normally, a contract will be signed before proceeding to the third phase when personnel are actually hired.

Phase 3 – Recruitment

The next phase contains the process of hiring – and perhaps firing – employees. As a rule, the buying organization, not the selling company, should handle any dismissals in order to avoid labour conflicts. Recruitment should be carried out following normal hiring procedures, the purpose of which is also to involve the employees as much as possible.

A typical recruitment process for transferring employees from the buying company to the selling company normally includes the following activities:

- Conducting individual interviews. The potential employee should, before the interview, fill out a form indicating his/her own strengths and weaknesses, job interests, special skills, etc.

- Offering guidance and support to the employees, e.g., implications of the new job situation.
- Putting employment agreements in place. In case of special union agreements, temporary measures may be allowed.
- Determining suitability of employee rotations and discharge provisions.

Phase 4 – Orientation and development

Now the hiring process is over, the employees start their new jobs at the selling company. In other words, they are now formal employees of the 'other' company, and the place of work is either at the client's premises or in the selling company's facilities. Also, individual career planning will begin. The tasks included in the orientation and development phase typically involve:

- Providing orientation courses to ensure that new employees develop an understanding of their new employer for relevance to the new work situation
- Examining the contract
- Devising methods/tools to be used in professional and personal development
- Designing and implementing training plans
- Facilitating networking to integrate the employees, both socially as well as professionally, into the company
- Initiating follow-up and individual discussions carried out on a regular basis with new employees to identify any problems after the transition.

Pitfalls and critical factors

Until now, the process of transferring employees in facilities management has been described in a rather simplified manner based largely on the experiences of an international facilities manager at IBM Denmark. However, companies engaging in these kinds of relations often encounter difficulties. The main sources of these difficulties can be summarized as follows:

- Lack of adequate preparation for the employee transfers because of insufficient cooperation between the two companies
- Animosity toward the selling company among transferred employees that adversely affects productivity
- Departure of key employees who do not wish to work for the selling company
- Ineffective integration of new employees into the corporate culture of the selling company
- Conflicts within the 'sales team' regarding employee transfers.

To avoid these potential problems the selling company's HR personnel must be able to engage in and handle the employee transfer process – they must play an active role. Typically the client's HR department is used only as a source of information on conditions of employment and the like.

As we have discussed above in general terms there are some critical factors to bear in mind in transferring employees:

- HR managers should be involved at the very beginning of the process.
- The transfer of employees should be customized to the situation and should not be treated as a routine one-size-fits-all exercise.
- Thorough preparation of the transfer groundwork should be undertaken as early as possible.
- Reliable and factual information should be made available to employees affected by the facilities management agreement.

- Employees should be involved as early as possible in the transfer process.
- HR policy should be made as attractive as possible to the transferred employees.
- Personal development should be emphasized as well as basic conditions of employment.
- Formal professional and social introductions should be used to make the new employee's integration into the new organization as smooth as possible.
- Training and development plans should be clearly delineated in order to be effective in the integration process.
- Follow-up should be undertaken after six months to provide a thorough debriefing of the employee transfer process.

Summary

The main aspects of 'transitioning' human resources presented in this chapter are highlighted below. At the root of most problems faced in seeking to change an organization's way of doing business is the difficulty of aligning the people involved in the intended change. The change involved in shifting human resources from one firm to another, although not necessarily entailing any concrete change in job content, is still an unsettling prospect for most people. As the IBM Denmark experience showed us, people cannot be dealt with as an afterthought in the facilities management selling process, nor treated as if they will approach the prospect of a 'transfer' in exactly the same way. Attention must be paid to laying the groundwork for the transfer even before the sales contract is finalized. It is especially critical to properly and responsibly communicate the intended change to the affected employees to minimize the risk of large-scale attrition as a consequence of weak communication strategies during the transition process. The recruitment and orientation of the newly hired employees sets the tone for long-term successful integration of these new members of the selling company's workforce and cannot be simply left to chance. All of these factors have been successfully incorporated into IBM Denmark's execution of 'employee transfer' that we believe provides a useful model and methodology for other firms facing similar challenges.

References

Breinstrup, T. 2004. Finsk telegigant udliciterer IT til IBM for 1.5 mia. kr. (A Finnish telecommunications giant outsources IT to IBM), *Berlingske Tidende*, 17 January, p. 9.

Burnes, B. 1992. *Managing change*, Pitman, London.

Jenster, P. V. and Pedersen, H. S. 1999. Deal maker or deal breaker: Human resources issues in successful outsourcing projects, *Journal of Strategic Change*, August, Vol. 8, pp. 263–268.

Maslow, A. 1943. A theory of human motivation, *Psychological Review*, Vol. 50, pp. 370–396 (reproduced in abridged form in Vroom, V. H. and Deci, E. L. 1970. *Management and motivation*, Penguin, Harmondsworth.

7 Structuring 'next generation' IT solutions

Introduction

In this chapter we examine the changing role of the traditional corporate IT department followed by an assessment of the problems that have characterized IT investments. Explanations for the costly failures of large numbers of IT projects – summarized as overadministration and undermanagement – are illustrated by specific examples. The remainder of the chapter looks in some detail at the rationale for establishing the 'next generation' IT solutions that more effectively enable process integration among buyers and sellers, thereby facilitating outsourcing activities.

The changing role of IT departments

The development of process integration between companies along the value chain would not be possible without extensive support of sophisticated IT systems. When companies engage in increasingly more complex outsourcing relationships, their interdependencies deepen and complex coordination, often in real time, must be available in order to make the integrated business processes work effectively and efficiently. As a consequence, the need for extensive support of IT systems for process integration has placed extreme pressure on IT departments in most companies. This extraordinary pressure arises from the fundamental change in focus in corporate

IT strategy – from the support of internal functions to the support of external processes – that follows the general trend toward process integration among companies.

As a direct result of the change in IT strategy focus, the technical complexity of IT systems and the related IT management have been raised to a level far beyond that which internal IT departments were originally intended to attain. At a time when the continuing structural development in most industries is characterized by the deepening of process integration along the value chain, the typical in-house IT department responsible for the delivery of IT support for business-critical process development appears to have been stretched beyond its capacity as evidenced by the large numbers of failed IT projects and the huge financial losses that they represent.

The real problem with IT investments

By the mid-1990s, it had become clear to most observers that there was something wrong in the way that most companies handled their IT investments judging from the high failure rates. Investigations into the problems revealed several issues (Strassmann, 1997; Davenport and Prusak, 1997). Clearly there were serious problems with the technology. In many organizations the proliferation of poorly coordinated client–server initiatives in the early 1990s had led to duplication of efforts in isolated departmental projects, resulting in serious incompatibility within corporate networks. The task of consolidating the fragmented corporate IT infrastructure was costly and, in many cases, very problematical because of the lack of relevant tools and technologies. Many technologies deployed in the early phases of the client–server era had not been properly tested before release and functioned suboptimally. Most of these problems could be traced back to the dramatic shift in the relations between IT vendors and customers that occurred in the early 1990s.

Before that shift the IT market was dominated by a handful of large, vertically intergrated vendors who marketed proprietary solutions to corporate customers. The vendors would control all aspects of the package including hardware, software and service, taking responsibility for the proper functioning of the entire package. Under this regime customers bought a specified 'functionality' and their risk associated with the underlying technology was limited. The downside to this regime was the unavoidable customer lock-in to a specific vendor and the lack of flexibility in terms of the functionality of the systems.

With the introduction of client–server technology in the early 1990s this market regime was challenged and surprisingly quickly overthrown by thousands of new, small and highly specialized IT vendors offering specialized products directly to corporate IT departments, or to business departments in many cases. Under this new market regime customers could pick and choose among competing hardware and software products and then assemble their own solutions often at a fraction of the cost of traditional solutions provided by the large vertically integrated vendor. For customers the potential upside was compelling: massive cost reductions, greater flexibility in functionality and integration of IT systems, significant reductions in customer lock-in and much faster development and implementation. However, these advantages came at a high price: customers took over the full risk associated with the proper functioning of their home-built solutions. No single vendor of any of the many different components that went into corporate solutions was prepared or positioned to make any guarantees about how the final solution would work or if it would work at all. Even today after more than 10 years of struggling with handling the risks associated with the client–server computing paradigm, many organization are still finding it difficult to strike the right balance between, on the one hand, the need for strict corporate IT standards in order to reduce the technological complexity and thereby the risks and, on the other hand, the business-related needs for business unit mangers to be able to exercise real power over what systems to implement and when to implement them in order to make IT investments business-driven. The purely technological issues associated with the management of IT should not be underestimated. However, the problems that organizations faced in the mid-1990s regarding the overall management of IT included both a variety of organizational issues and a large component of complicated risk management.

What ROI?

Under these circumstances the high failure rate of large IT projects should come as no surprise. The task of developing and implementing new management processes to effectively control the increasingly complex corporate IT agenda would necessarily take years to accomplish. To complicate things even further, the efforts that most organizations put into this process was, in effect, aiming at a moving target. New technologies were being introduced continually and they opened up new and compelling opportunities for various business departments. What was surprising was the lack of discipline in the financial resource allocation for IT projects. During the 1990s IT investments in many industries grew to 10% or more of revenues. Nonetheless, even IT projects considered to be highly strategic were often launched without any systematic analysis of the expected return on the investment. For some reason, IT-related investment decisions were treated differently than almost any other type of corporate investment.

Several studies of corporate investments in Enterprise Resource Planning (ERP) systems that took place since the mid-1990s reveal that investment decisions – often in the order of tens of millions of dollars – were made without any clear understanding of the costs that the total implementation process would involve or how and when this investment would give a positive return to the company. In one of these studies, the German research company Nucleus Research (2003) found that 57% of SAP customers interviewed did not believe that they had achieved a positive ROI after having used their SAP applications for an average of 2.8 years. The study, which was based on interviews with SAP project managers and senior managers in 21 large organization in various industries, found that many SAP customers had not even defined a process for evaluating ROI on their investments in SAP projects for which an average initial cost of deployment was more than $10 million.

If strategic IT investment decisions like major ERP roll-outs were made based on such relatively loose assumptions about their economic value, as the Nucleus Research study indicates, it becomes more understandable that the many smaller and tactical departmental IT investments were often founded more on fashion and industry hype than on traditional cost–benefit analysis. According to one research report published in 1995 by The Standish Group (1995) American companies and government agencies out of a total software development budget of $250 billion 'will spend $81 billion for cancelled software projects. These same organization will pay an additional $59 billion for software projects that will be completed, but will exceed their original time estimates.' Of the estimated 175 000 large software development projects in process in 1995 only 16% were delivered on time and on budget and as much as 31% of the projects were cancelled some time during the development phase. Although a high failure rate might be expected for some projects that involved the use of new and untested technology, many of the projects included in the Standish analysis were 'as mundane as a driver's license database, a new accounting package, or an order entry system'.

IT: Overadministrated and undermanaged

Why is IT so poorly managed that the waste of financial resources on failed IT development projects amounts to an estimated $100 billion or more on a yearly basis in the USA alone?

Since the mid-1990s the search for an answer to this question from both commercial research companies and academic research institutions has focused on the difficulties associated with aligning IT with organizational cultures, on the lack of user involvement in design and development processes and on the lack of precise mapping of the actual business processes that the systems are intended to support. Most studies also emphasize the importance of senior management's active involvement in strategic IT decisions. This research clearly has had an impact on the management of IT in most organizations.

Today's organizations have an overwhelming number of IT committees that involve so-called 'end-users' and 'business sponsors' at every level in the decisions and the design of almost all corporate IT development projects. Senior management can no longer avoid taking an active role in the formulation of corporate IT strategy, and in most cases large IT projects must be presented in a cost–benefit perspective for funding approval. Apparently everything is done to comply with the lessons learned during the early 1990s. Nonetheless, despite these efforts, the failure rate of large IT projects and the resulting financial losses are still significant.

In a study from 2002 about the success of large Customer Relationship Management (CRM) projects researchers from McKinsey found that in general terms at least 60% of the projects did not meet the expectations of managers responsible for the investment decisions (Ebner *et al.*, 2002). In terms of functionality several key functions had been defined during the decision process, but in 65% of the cases the systems did not meet expectations in any one of the key functions measured.

On the financial side the expected revenue growth and other expected advantages had not been realized. In some industry sectors 80% of CRM projects failed to provide any contribution to economic performance. A large proportion of the projects missed deadlines and cost overruns of 200 to 300% were not unusual.

In the case of CRM projects, most senior managers did take an active role, simply because the projects were extremely costly. In the late 1990s companies around the world spent a total of $3.5 billion a year on CRM software. The total cost of CRM projects has been estimated to be three to five times that amount. According to the McKinsey study, a large-scale corporate CRM project would typically cost the company around $100 million and take three years to implement. Today hundreds of CRM systems sit idle and unused on corporate networks and all involved wonder what went wrong. The answers that came up in both the McKinsey study and in the previously mentioned Nucleus Research study about ERP project failures are strikingly similar to the answers in the analysis of the mid-1990s: a lack of clearly defined objectives, weak organizational alignment and technical problems.

In 2002 the problems related to business alignment, and more broadly to organizational and cultural alignment, are no longer rooted in a lack of end-user involvement, business sponsor involvement or, for that matter, the involvement of senior management. Everyone appears to be heavily involved, but in many cases with the unintended result that the IT project designs become burdened with hundreds of 'special needs' that require complicated and costly customization. In this process a relatively low-risk project for implementing a standard system gradually evolves into a high-risk development project. The technical problems also looked different in 2002.

During the late 1990s most organizations managed to bring order to their IT infrastructure and, in general terms, the typical corporate network of 2002 was well managed and under control. However, the large IT projects of the late 1990s, such as ERP, CRM and procurement, were no longer focused only on the support of internal business functions connected to the corporate network. Instead, they were aiming to support a broad range of complicated business processes taking place among separate organizations: suppliers, distributors and customers (Häcki and Lighton, 2001). With this change in scope the technical complexity grew exponentially. As the numbers above indicate, most corporate IT departments were unable to meet this new challenge. Even in light of the magnitude of the financial losses related to the typical in-house corporate IT projects, the most serious problem with the shortcomings of IT departments is lost opportunities for the further development of deeper and more automated process integration among companies (Butler *et al.*, 1997).

The IT paradox

IT must be regarded as a most important enabler of the process integration among companies that actually does take place in most industries. Yet, at the same time, it is probably one of the most important inhibitors to realizing further business opportunities based on IT. When looked at in more detail, this apparent paradox is not difficult to resolve. The IT that 'enables' is the IT functionality that actually works in the form of IT systems and the related IT infrastructure, whereas the IT that 'inhibits' is the institutional framework for producing the relevant functionality centered on the typical corporate IT department.

From a purely theoretical standpoint the obvious solution to this situation is to introduce changes to the institutional framework for the production of IT functionality in such a way as to secure the availability of the relevant functionality for further business development at the lowest cost possible. Since the late 1990s IT suppliers – from the leading global players such as IBM and HP to a myriad of new and often smaller companies – have developed technologies and business processes that have been aiming at this rather obvious opportunity to support further development of process integration among companies. Most of these seller-driven initiatives have been limited in scope and have been focusing on delivering new tools to help the traditional IT department solve isolated and specific technical issues. By following this approach successful suppliers could get immediate access to the corporate IT budget controlled mainly by the IT department.

Although some of the products and services actually solved a number of specific internal problems, they did not address the more fundamental problem of the institutional framework for the production of IT functionality. The more important initiatives among suppliers did deal directly with this institutional framework. These initiatives were simultaneously aiming at providing customers with access to new technology designed to support process integration among companies and at making the technology available within a radically different institutional framework to substantially lower the risk of developing, implementing and operating the technology (Wainewright, 1999; Wendland, 1999; Holincheck, 1999; Cameron, 1999; IDC, 1999; Whiting, 1999). These initiatives took on many different forms in terms of the specific approach to the technical delivery mechanism and to the proposed contractual framework, but most of the solutions had some key elements in common:

- Centrally operated outside the customer's IT environment
- Based on highly standardized solutions with only limited options for customer-specific customization
- Built and delivered to customers based on standard Internet protocols
- Priced on a combination of a set-up fee and some variation of metering of actual usage and/or the number of active user accounts.

Given the very high risk profile of the traditional institutional framework built around the corporate IT department, these kind of so-called *Application Service Provider* (ASP) solutions could be expected to be embraced by corporate managers. The solutions offered under the ASP model would substantially reduce the capital outlay for new IT systems; the systems would be available almost instantly; system integration to suppliers and customers was built in and immediately available when needed and there was only relatively little risk involved in relation to the availability of the systems. For most of the pioneering ASP vendors who introduced this kind of solution the reality of the market situation turned out to be disappointing. Despite many attractive features to the solutions in terms of functionality and delivery framework very few vendors managed to convince enough customers to engage in a change process of the dominant institutional framework for the production of IT functionality. Only through a long and costly process of further development of the business proposition have some of the original vendors managed to bring about the deep structural change that is associated with the development and introduction of a new institutional framework for the production of IT functionality.

One characteristic of this further development is its typical combination of traditional outsourcing with the standardization features and metering pricing mechanisms that were among the key features of the first-generation offerings. This approach represents a tall order for most vendors and one of the characteristic elements of the new line of next generation offerings is that the field is totally dominated by a handful of large global players, such as IBM, HP and CSC.

The 'next generation' approach to IT

With this broadening of the scope of the offerings to include not only the delivery of new systems but also the takeover of the operations and management of large elements or even the entire existing IT installation, the leading sellers have found a formula that so far has proved to have sufficient appeal to some, primarily large, corporate customers. Although the number of contracts for these 'next generation' solutions is still rather limited, the size and the strategic significance of many of the deals are sufficiently compelling to be regarded as a structural trend that can be expected to be gradually accepted as a norm in most market segments.

As this change process unfolds the appearance of a new institutional framework for the production of IT – the formation of a new 'dominant design' for IT functionality – can be anticipated. In this new institutional framework the traditional in-house IT department has only a limited – if any – role. It is likely that the development of this new institutional framework should be expected to follow along the same lines as for other areas of process integration among companies, namely standardization, specialization and the exchange of processes in the form of solutions rather than simply products or specific services.

The primary driver for this development will be the need for companies to reduce the risk associated with the further development of process integration and automation, both of which are dependent on the availability of still more sophisticated IT support. Since the financial and overall competitive gains of further process integration and automation hold huge potential the driving force should be regarded as sufficiently strong to bring about the transition in the institutional framework that surrounds the production of IT functionality, at least in the long run. The barriers to change in the institutional framework can be expected to be associated mainly with the formulation and operationalization of the associated legal and contractual framework.

Building on the understanding by R. H. Coase (1937) regarding the logic defining the functions that a company chooses to carry out in-house and those that it chooses to acquire through marketplace transactions, the case for a landslide move in the IT arena toward market transactions is overwhelming when viewed in purely economic terms. However, this landslide move is not materializing. Following Coasean logic, the reason lies in the difficulties associated with establishing a broadly accepted legal and contractual framework for the market-based transactions as well as in the organizational inertia that makes it possible for established constituencies within organizations to resist changes despite financial evidence to the contrary. The combined legal and social costs of moving to a market-based transaction for the production of IT functionality seem to constitute a substantial inhibitor in the development of a new and more rational institutional framework. By studying a number of cases where these barriers have been overcome it appears clear that some of the greatest difficulties are related to the special nature of the relationship among the parties in the transactions.

When the production of IT functionality is transformed from being an in-house company function to being a commercial transaction among individual companies, a type of relationship is being established that cannot be understood as a normal buyer/supplier relationship. The reason is fairly straightforward. In today's organization IT represents, to a large extent, a vital tool for ongoing business development as well as a company-specific electronic 'frequency' that carries not only data but also important cultural elements and values. One of the most important drivers leading an organization to opt for a market-based transaction in this area is the desire to reduce the risk associated with further development of the IT support necessary for new business processes vital for a company's core business. In other words, moving from a traditional in-house production of IT functionality to an institutional framework based on market transactions is usually done as an element in a much broader strategic reorientation of the company's business focus. By moving the production of IT functionality into a market-based transaction regime, the customer expects to achieve not only cost reductions but also, and equally important, an improved position toward realizing key business objectives that in itself might have very little to do with IT.

Although the move toward an institutional framework based on market transactions for the production of IT functionality can be explained within the logical framework suggested by Coase, the difficulties associated with the operationalization of an institutional framework in this particular area have to do with the nature of the relationship between buyer and seller. In this case, it must necessarily take the form of a deep and long-term relationship in which only some elements, and not necessarily the most important elements seen from the buyer's perspective, are specific enough to be defined in classical contractual terms. In legal terms the buyer and the seller remain within the framework of the traditional notion of the individual 'firm', as the term is used by Coase, and much of the logic that drives the development of a new institutional framework can be explained in the context of transaction costs. However, the relationships created within the framework of 'next generation' IT solutions constitute a level of partnership that blurs the traditional distinction between in-house and market-based transactions.

The contractual framework that guides the market-based transactions will tend to include elements that relate to the general business objectives of the buyer and may include provisions regarding pricing that, to some extent, are tied to successful achievement of those business objectives. In these cases, the seller must have a certain degree of influence on the management decisions of the buyer organization in order to fulfil the contract. Without such influence, the seller has no means of securing the proper functioning of those elements in the contract that relate to some defined business objectives on which the payment to the seller is at least partly defined.

In some of the areas that relate to the achievement of defined business objectives of the buyer organization the buyer and the seller must engage in a form of shared management responsibility in order to make the contractual arrangement work. Even if this management aspect of the relationship is not specified in the contract, as in the case of the seller delivering management consulting and training to the buyer organization, the reality of the business relationship is that both buyer and seller must be willing and able to actively share responsibility in some area of management within the buying organization. By doing so, the relationship takes on a format that is new in relation to the distinction between in-house and market-based transactions as defined by Coase. According to Coase the crucial difference between in-house and market-based transactions is that the in-house transactions are guided by management decisions while the market-based transactions are guided by a combination of the pricing mechanism and the institutional framework that regulates commercial transactions in the particular industry. As sketched out in the above line of argument this understanding of the border between the firm and the market is being challenged by the type of relationships associated with the continued deepening of process integration among companies along the value chain.

According to Coase the crucial difference between in-house and market-based transactions is that in-house transactions are guided by management decisions, whereas market-based transactions are guided by a combination of the pricing mechanism and the institutional framework regulating commercial transactions in the particular industry. As sketched out in the above line of argument, deepening process integration along the value chain is continually challenging firm/market boundaries.

The difficulties of precisely defining the buyer/seller relationship in legal contracts and of handling the shared management responsibility for the framework to be operational and beneficial to both parties are reflected in the resistance to widespread adoption of this institutional framework built on market-based transactions.

From an outsourcing perspective, fragmentation of activities to realize the economies of scale and scope arising from larger and more professionally managed activities, is nowhere more predominant than in IT and telecommunication services. Firms continuing to retain IT services in-house must realize that such decisions come with a significant competitive disadvantage.

Summary

In drawing conclusions on the structuring of 'next generation' IT solutions there are several points that should be highlighted.

First, it is important to recognize that many of the problems associated with IT development projects can be attributed to a lack of clearly defined objectives, to weak organizational alignment and to technical problems.

Second, it is important to recognize that IT can be both an enabler and an inhibitor of process integration – it enables by the IT systems and related infrastructure that it provides and it inhibits by the institutional framework that characterizes the typical corporate IT department.

Third, it is important to recognize that the main driver for companies to outsource the IT function lies in risk reduction – reducing the risks associated with further development of process integration and automation, both of which necessitate increasingly sophisticated IT support.

Fourth, it is important to recognize that retaining IT services in-house can lead to significant competitive disadvantages arising from the loss of the economies of scale and scope that are available from specialist IT suppliers.

References

Butler, P., Hall, T. W., Hanna, A. M., Mendonca, L., Auguste, B., Manyika, J. and Sahay, A. 1997. A revolution in interaction, *The McKinsey Quarterly*, No. 1.

Cameron, B. 1999. Driving IT's externalisation, *The Forrester Report*, January.

Coase, R. H. 1937. The nature of the firm, *Economica*, Vol. 4, pp. 386–405.

Davenport, T. H. and Prusak, L. 1997. *Information ecology: Mastering the information and knowledge environment*, Oxford University Press, Oxford.

Ebner, M., Hu, A., Levitt, D. and McCrory, J. 2002. How to rescue CRM, *The McKinsey Quarterly*, No. 4.

Häcki, R. and Lighton, J. 2001. The future of the networked company, *The McKinsey Quarterly*, No. 3.

Holincheck, J. 1999. ASP Vendor overview, Giga Information Group, November.

IDC 1999. IDC forecast high-end application service provider market will reach $2 billion by 2003, March.

Nucleus Research 2003. The real ROI from SAP.

The Standish Group 1995. CHAOS©.

Strassmann, P. A. 1997. *The squandered computer: Evaluating the business alignment of information technologies*, The Information Economics Press.

Wainewright, P. 1999. Anatomy of an ASP: Computing's new genus, ASPnews.com, August.

Wendland, R. 1999. Application Service Providers, *Durlarcher Research*, July.

Whiting, R. 1999. Software morphs into a service, *Information Week*, October.

8 Achieving quality in outsourcing

Introduction

In this chapter we explore the role of managing quality in terms of facilitating the delivery of higher quality products and services to the buyer and also the creation of greater profits for the supplier of outsourcing solutions. The delivery of better products and services may, in turn, enhance the profitability of the buyer's business activities leading to enhanced business opportunities for the supplier in the future. Definitions of quality are continually adjusted over time as a result of interaction between the buyer and the seller. In the outsourcing relationship buyers and sellers may jointly define quality standards for the outsourced service on an ongoing basis.

Understanding the role of quality management

Outsourcing has evolved into new forms. One difference between the older and newer forms of outsourcing is the move from the sale of *separately identifiable physical products or services* to *integrated supplies* comprising physical products, service components, know-how and, quite often, managerial responsibility. Quality is much easier to define and measure for a specific component, such as production of standardized bolts, or a peripheral service, such as cleaning in office buildings. It is no less important for integrated supplies, but much more complex and difficult to define.

Contracts for integrated supplies differ significantly from the traditional sale of products and services on numerous dimensions – complexity, demand for coordination and integration, control mechanisms and buyer/vendor relationships (Jenster *et al.*, 1994; Ketelhöhn, 1992; Everett, 1990). As companies outsource, issues revolving around quality and quality management become even more pivotal. Once outsourcing has taken place, the buying company is dependent on the selling company for the quality of the outsourced solution; without sustained high quality of the outsourced function, the quality of the buyer's own products and services will suffer adverse consequences.

Earlier we gave the example of Railtrack, the engineering company that owns the railway tracks, signalling, stations and related assets in Great Britain. Maintenance of the system is outsourced to various independent companies. Jarvis plc, an infrastructure company, holds the contract for the east coast main line. When there was a serious rail crash caused by key bolts being removed from some points that resulted in some passenger deaths, the issue of quality performance came to the fore. Jarvis argued that it was sabotage, although there is a widespread belief that it was a quality issue. It requires little imagination to see the damage that such a high-profile case causes to the reputations of both organizations and there have been resultant changes in the way Railtrack monitors the quality performance of its contractors.

The Public Record Office, the UK's national archive, had its high reputation tarnished by the performance of an outsourcing partner. One of its numerous activities is the national census and the enumerators' returns for the 1901 census were due for release on 1 January 2002. Previous versions had been microfilmed and the public was able to consult these files. Name indexes were largely developed by the voluntary sector and they lagged behind the release of the microfilms. For the 1901 census the Public Record Office decided to arrange for public access through a website and to have a name index available from the outset. Fees were charged for the downloading of information beyond a basic level. The project was outsourced and historians of various types, including the numerous individuals involved in local and family history, were poised to begin to access the website. The system collapsed on the first day under the weight of enquiries and even nine months later the Public Record Office still was not able to reopen the service and fulfil its obligation to make the information available after 100 years. This is not simply a matter of teething problems, but a more fundamental quality issue – the scheme did not work because the system was seriously flawed and did not operate effectively.

How then does the seller – the supplier – of outsourced services manage quality to prevent problems for the buyer? In what ways is the seller's quality management system affected because it is delivering a part of the buyer's production process?

One way to look at outsourcing and quality management is the European Foundation for Quality Management (EFQM) Excellence Model (www.efqm.org). The EFQM is an organization that has been helping European businesses for more than a decade to make better products and to deliver better services. The EFQM Excellence Model provides a general approach to understanding the dimensions in a company's quality management system. It is based on nine criteria, five of which are so-called enablers that represent the actual work of the company and four are results that represent the achievements of the company. The results cover the organization's achievements through the enablers. The nine criteria, as shown in Figure 8.1, constitute the basis against which an organization can assess its progress toward excellence.

This Excellence Model, which is linked to the annual awarding of the European Quality Award, builds on a Total Quality Management (TQM) philosophy (Neergaard, 1997) and therefore also reflects the

The enablers: Leadership

People

Policy and strategy

Partnerships and resources

Processes

The results: People results

Customers results

Society results

Key performance results

Enablers lead to results and results should lead to innovation and learning in organizations.

Figure 8.1 – The enabler and result criteria based on the EFQM Excellence Model (the EFQM Excellence Model was devised by the European Foundation for Quality Management).

fact that TQM in organizational settings has expanded to embrace a wider palette of organizational affairs. This means that quality management is assessed not only in relation to delivery of products and services, but also in relation to the various ways in which the organization satisfies the needs of its stakeholders, be they customers, employees, society at large, or shareholders. A feature highlighted by the Excellence Model – and one of the changes in the 2000 version of the model – is the concept of partnerships and *how external partnerships are managed*.

The traditional writings on TQM (e.g., Deming, 1986) strongly advocate building long-term relationships with suppliers. However, the Excellence Model extends the concept of partnerships beyond a focus simply on suppliers to include customers as well in the management of external partnerships, a consideration of relevance for outsourcing relationships. Our interest focuses on the 'partnerships and resources' criterion – specifically the impact on the seller's quality management – and how it affects the other model criteria. We now turn to the more practical implications of outsourcing from the supplier's point of view. We attempt to identify some of the quality management challenges imposed by outsourcing on the supplier and relate those challenges to the Excellence Model.

Defining quality for integrated products and services

Very often today a salient feature of outsourcing is 'bundling', combinations of both products and services. Combination is a logical consequence of the fact that a particular task is no longer taken care of in-house. If, for instance, a company outsources a production process, then the surrounding support functions such as ordering, handling and delivery will have to be managed, or at least coordinated, by the supplier. For the supplier, the implication is that it no longer only delivers the given production part but now also has to make sure that the production part is properly coordinated with, and integrated into, the buyer's production process. To illustrate this point we will look at an example taken from a major international textile company with a divisional structure. The company renders services ranging from cleaning to rental services involving the takeover of a client's textile inventory.

This textile industry example presents the case of two customers who have outsourced their entire 'textile function' (Pedersen, 2000). The first customer is a large company involved in passenger sea travel in the tourist industry. The second customer is an international hotel chain. In the interviews at these two companies, both interviewees were asked to list and rank all of the parameters on which they measured quality. The rankings by the two interviewees are shown in Figure 8.2 with the white columns representing the perspectives of the sea travel company and the grey

Dimensions on which quality is measured	Relevance of quality categories to customers Relevant = Yes Not relevant = No		Importance to customers 1= not important 4 = very important	
	Yes/No	Yes/No	1–4	1–4
Cleanliness	Yes	Yes	4	4
Agreed quantity	Yes	Yes	4	4
Timely delivery	Yes	Yes	4	4
Logistics capacity	Yes	Yes	4	2
Quality of the physical product	Yes	Yes	4	4
Environmentally friendly production	No	Yes	—	3
Environmentally friendly for users	Yes	Yes	3	3
Price	Yes	Yes	3	4
Width of product/service line	No	Yes	—	3
Product development	No	Yes	—	4
Understanding of our business	Yes	Yes	4	4
Documentation to our customers	No	No	—	—
Dialogue	Yes	Yes	4	3
Dedication	Yes	Yes	4	3
Openness	Yes	No	4	—
Advice on use and consumption	No	Yes	—	3
Information on market development, etc.	Yes	Yes	2	2
Administrative capacity, invoicing, etc.	Yes	Yes	4	3
Quick responsiveness to complaints	Yes	Yes	4	4
Services in general	Yes	No	4	—
Other: Delivery according to specifications	Yes	—	4	—
Other: Notice if deviations from the agreed	Yes	—	4	—

Figure 8.2 – Defining quality. (Source: Pedersen, 2000).

columns representing the perspectives of the international hotel chain.

No statistical methods have been applied to test the relationship between the various dimensions or background information such as total budget, the duration of contracts and their size. The list is intended to identify precisely the quality dimensions. As can be seen from the ranking in the table, the two customers evaluated quality on a wide range of dimensions. These dimensions varied from the 'traditional' ones such as price, delivery and quality of the product, which are relatively easy to measure and define, to the more 'qualitative' ones such as dialogue and dedication. The latter dimensions can be directly compared to the seller's ability to manage partnerships. In between these two dimensions we find dimensions that relate to aspects of understanding the customer's business and administrative capacity. The differences in the weighting given to the dimensions by the two customers are interesting. Both appear to have given high priority to the traditional dimensions, but otherwise they had highly individual preferences and clearly evaluated quality differently.

To define customer needs and expectations in terms of quality is not new – it is a very central aspect in TQM. However, no clear and unifying definition of quality exists in the literature. Several scholars have tried to provide an overview and categorize the different definitions and understandings of quality. Examples of such overviews are Neergaard (1997), who identifies four definitions, Hansen (1996), who operates with five definitions, and Reeves and Bednar (1994), who distinguish among four definitions.

The various discussions of quality definitions show that no single definition of quality exists which, in turn, further underlines the need for defining quality in relation to the individual customer. In relation to outsourcing, the particular aspect, as illustrated in Figure 8.2, seems to be the wide range of dimensions on which customers judge quality.

In sum, the definition of quality and the dimensions influencing it are apparently highly individualized and relationship-specific or contextual, and thus quality needs to be defined separately in each relationship. As noted, similarities do exist among the customers, notably in relation to the core product or service, but the other dimensions and the weights attached to them can only be defined in the individual relationship. In both traditional and outsourcing relationships, the range of dimensions on which customers judge quality is wide. The challenge for the seller is then to identify and operationalize the relevant dimensions for each customer. However, customers do not seem to have systems in place for measuring quality or all relevant dimensions (Pedersen, 2002). The customers for the product/service, who indeed do measure quality and the performance of their supplier, mostly measure the harder, more quantifiable aspects, although the softer dimensions are also important to their perception of quality. To a large extent the same also applies to sellers. In general, the systems for monitoring quality are to a high degree evolving around the core product and/or service.

In his research on quality in outsourcing relationships Pedersen (2002) found that definitions of quality were continually adjusted over the course of the buying/selling relationship and that definitions of quality tended to be jointly developed on the basis of inter-organizational learning. The principal challenges related to quality that the seller of outsourcing solutions faces based on the Excellence Model enablers – challenges involving leadership and strategy, challenges involving processes and challenges involving people – are addressed below.

Challenges: Leadership and strategy

Several implications for leadership in the selling company arise from the discussion of outsourcing relations in practice. Outsourcing involves entering into new ways of doing business both in terms of the buying company's relations with customers and also in terms of the products or services delivered. This is an important aspect for management in the selling organization to recognize. Externally, it means that the company's relationship with its customers is changing. The seller has taken over more functions or tasks than was previously the case. As mentioned above, in order to deliver a part of another company's production process necessarily means that the seller will have to execute or coordinate some of the related support functions.

At least two consequences can be identified. One is the need for sellers to clearly identify what is being outsourced, a task that includes determining the related support functions in the buying firm. A second consequence is that buyers must recognize exactly what they are buying, a task that requires the seller to communicate the precise details to the buyer. As buyers' definitions of quality expand, no longer do they judge only the more professional skills of the supplier related to the hard aspects of the services or products, such as freedom from defects, timely delivery and cleanliness. Now the more personal and softer qualities, such as service orientation, dedication and dialogue, take on much greater importance for buyers. These softer qualities require sellers to have competencies in partnership-building, competencies involving effective functioning in networks of relationships for which trust and commitment play a central role.

In addition, clear understanding of the quality requirements for the outsourced service within the seller's company is also important. The internal 'selling' regarding the quality to be delivered appears to be a task that deserves managerial attention and one that is inseparably linked to effective delivery of outsourcing. Whenever a company decides to take over parts of the buying company's production process, it should also carefully consider the internal requirements, specifically the necessity of internal communication strategies. If internal communication is not a priority for the selling company, then the consequences could very well be that it will not live up to the buying company's expectations of quality.

In general terms, the challenge is to design a system that takes both the internal and external aspects of the organization into account because the significance of these two facets is accentuated by outsourcing. From the Excellence Model perspective, a stronger emphasis on communication, internally and externally, would address this leadership and strategy challenge.

Challenges: Processes

The research by Pedersen (2002) points to the increase of documentation related to quality management for outsourced products and services over time. The companies doing the outsourcing appear to become increasingly demanding about quality management aspects such as documentation as they gain more experience in outsourcing and as their outsourcing relationships mature; hence, they tend to put greater weight on the documentation related to quality management by the supplier. In the early stages buyers may not totally realize the full scope of what they are outsourcing and how it relates to the quality that they deliver to their customers. We suggest that this finding indicates the importance for sellers to document their ability to manage quality in the early stages of the relationship. From an internal perspective, documentation serves to make tacit knowledge on the part of the relationship manager explicit. This situation could indicate scope for proactive action by the seller with respect to quality management in the initial phases of the outsourcing.

Another aspect of processes relates to the takeover of employees, previously discussed in Chapter 6, in terms of process documentation. As noted under challenges to leadership and strategy, a central issue involves identification of what is actually being outsourced and isolation of the various elements in order to define the task precisely. That particular challenge is accentuated when the selling company, in identifying and documenting the task, has to rely on employees in the buying company. The rationale is that the seller must convince the buyer that the outsourced solutions provided are superior to in-house options. This objective relies on careful articulation of the benefits offered and their documentation. For the employees being transferred from the buying firm to the selling firm the challenge is to document what they have been doing previously.

Challenges: People

This section focuses on challenges related to people management in the Excellence Model. The main focus, however, is not on how to manage people in the seller's company, but rather on the stages prior to employment of the transferring employees. People can be an important quality dimension in outsourcing. Considerations of the potential supplier's HR policy may come into play when deciding whether, if at all, to outsource a certain function. Nevertheless, the transfer of employees seems to be a much ignored aspect of outsourcing as we argued at the outset of this book in Chapter 1.

At least two important conclusions can be derived from these observations. The first is that attention should be paid to laying the groundwork for the transfer before the sales contract is finalized in order to prepare for the actual transfer and integration of the new employees before they are in the 'People' box of the Excellence Model, so to speak. The second conclusion is that HR issues may be an important element in the buying company's perception of quality, particularly in terms of whether or not the selling company has an HR policy that it considers to be attractive and reassuring to its former employees.

Factors conditioning quality management

We offer several recommendations on useful quality management strategies in response to the challenges posed by outsourcing. Because quality is defined on a wide range of dimensions and outsourcing poses new challenges to the seller's quality management system it is often difficult to identify appropriate management strategies for quality. Empirical evidence shows that over time outsourcing is moving towards critical and strategic functions, including product development and finance. Quality is important in any outsourcing arrangement, but the vulnerability of the buyer increases with the critical or strategic nature of the function that is outsourced. Bad quality may include defects and missing items from deliveries, lateness and poor attitudes of the seller's personnel, particularly when dealing with the buyer's customers. We might also add safety to our list of vulnerability factors. Outsourced maintenance of an office may result mainly in inconvenience, if quality is not managed; however, much more than inconvenience is involved if a badly maintained air conditioning system leads to an outbreak of Legionnaires' disease. Poor cleaning may not have disastrous consequences in most situations, but the repercussions are highly significant if the contract is for cleaning a hospital.

Our conclusion is that the requirements for quality management increase as the buyer's vulnerability increases. As we mentioned earlier, research results indicate that buyers also seem to put more emphasis on documented quality management over time, but this finding is likely to be a reflection of a lack of understanding when contracts are first put into place. This dimension could be 'coupled' with the aspect of complexity of the outsourced function, meaning how multidimensional and measurable it is. Again, complexity can be either high or low. The decisive factor of determining complexity may be how capable the customer is in defining quality. The more capable the supplier is, the more specification-specific or standardized its quality management system will be.

As shown in the textile industry example, customers are able to control and specify what they are buying based on factors such as price, delivery, size and weight, all of which make quality relatively unambiguous. The customer can check on these quality measures on delivery, whereas with dimensions such as dedication and dialogue it is more difficult to define quality measures. In some situations, such as the example from the textile industry mentioned above, outsourcing also contains an important element of product development. In other words, an outsourcing service may be composed of elements from both ends of the scale. The existence of dimensions such as product development indicates that the supplier's quality management system must be able to document not only ability to deliver the agreed outsourcing deliverables but also to secure constant improvement of them.

Following this line of argument, the less able the buyer is to define quality, the more 'open-ended' the supplier's quality management system will need to be, meaning that the need for the supplier to define quality is greater. This situation arises primarily because of the absence of benchmarks that might indicate, in turn, the need for even closer relations between seller and buyer, or the need for the buyer to maintain personnel in-house who can match those of the seller in terms of knowledge and expertise. It does not mean that some of the elements in the quality management system cannot be standardized. At the lower end of the complexity continuum, the personnel receiving or handling the services delivered, as in the case of the matron in a hotel, may be sufficient to ensure that the basic quality checks are carried out.

Figure 8.3 shows a framework based on two key factors shaping quality management in outsourcing relationships. In this framework the outsourced function, and hence the buyers, can be categorized using the dimensions of closeness or importance to the core activities of the buyer and of complexity of the outsourced function or sellers' scope to define quality.

The framework has been filled out to illustrate some overall characteristics of the role of quality management in each category. The basic idea is that the role of quality management will vary according to category. If customers display the combination low/low in the matrix, then they are fully capable of defining what they are buying and sellers must document that they can meet these requirements. If, however, the customer has the combination high/high, then the

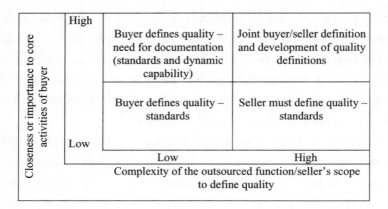

Figure 8.3 – Quality management in outsourcing relationships. (Source: Pedersen, 2002).

need for the seller to specifically define and operationalize quality is greater because the buyer may not be in a position to fully grasp the complexity. However, the seller must convince the buyer that the necessary quality will be delivered and will continue to be delivered which, in turn, requires in-depth knowledge of customer's operations and hence joint development of quality standards.

Effective partnership relationships may be able to contribute significantly to development of tailored solutions offering greater efficiency and hence cost savings for the buyer that the supplier may, in turn, be able to pass on to other customers to garner better returns on its investment in producing this customized solution.

Summary

Managing quality in the delivery of outsourcing solutions focuses on how efficiency and profitability can be increased in relationships between buyers and sellers through specific strategies to manage quality. First, it is critical to clearly define what is being sold by the seller to the buyer, including the consequences of suboptimal quality on the operations of the buyer so that the buyer's expectations can be defined and managed. Second, it is important to recognize that quality needs to take into account the activities that are occurring between the seller's company and the buyer's company as well as those activities wholly occurring within the selling company; higher levels of similarity between the product/service provided by the seller and the core activities of the buyer require higher levels of relationship structuring in terms of, for example, frequency of meetings, to ensure that supplier performance meets buyer requirements. Third, it is important to use the initial buyer/seller discussions to manage the buyer's expectations about costs as often buyers anticipate that there will be significant cost savings possible through the outsourcing arrangements whether this is economically feasible or not in terms of the quality expectations. Fourth, it is important to monitor quality carefully over the duration of the contractual relationship because quality is continuously adjusted along the way through interaction: in outsourcing relationships quality is often jointly developed.

References

Deming, W. E. 1986. *Out of the crisis*, Massachusetts Institute of Technology, Cambridge, MA.

Everett, M. 1990. Systems integrators: Marketing's new maestros, *Sales and Marketing Management*, November 1990, pp. 50–60.

Hansen, T. 1996. Kvalitetsbegrebet i samfundsvidenskaberne, *Samfundsøkonomen*, Oktober 1996:2, pp. 20–26.

Jenster, P., Kettelhöhn, W. and Kassman, B. 1994. IBM Branch Office – Irgendvoe, Austria, Selling solutions, in Vandermerwe, S. and Lovelock, C. (eds), *Competing though services – Strategy and implementation*, Prentice Hall, New York, pp. 149–165.

Ketelhöhn, W. 1992. Solutions selling, *European Management Journal*, Vol. 10, No. 1, pp. 10–21.

Neergaard, P. 1997. *Kvalitetsstyring? En undersøgelse i danske virksomheder*, Jurist- og Økonomforbundets Forlag, København.

Pedersen, H. S. 2000. Outsourcing and quality management: some implications and challenges – a supplier's perspective, in *Proceedings of the 3rd International Conference on Building People and Organisational Excellence*, 20–22 August, Aarhus School of Business, pp. 518–529.

Pedersen, H. S. 2002. Quality management in outsourcing relationships – Framing a supplier's perspective, PhD Series, 2002:19, Samfundslitteratur, Copenhagen, Denmark.

Reeves, C. A. and Bednar D. A. 1994. Defining quality: Alternatives and implications, *Academy of Management Review*, Vol. 19, No. 3, pp. 419–445.

www.efqm.org Reference for European Foundation for Quality Management Excellence Model.

9 Getting a good slice of a larger pie

Introduction

In this final chapter we review the topic of outsourcing specifically in terms of the central question in profitable business outsourcing: *Can money be made from the new relationship opportunities?* To answer this question we look at outsourcing as a pie from both the seller's perspective and from the buyer's perspective. In both cases there is the potential to obtain a larger slice of the pie and also the potential for making the pie larger.

The outsourcing pie

Each party to an outsourcing contract of any type enters the transaction in the belief that it is in its own commercial interests. If we imagine the buyer's business as a pie, the supplier initially seeks to take a slice from the pie. Other suppliers, employees and fiscal authorities take other slices, along with a host of other pie eaters, leaving (one hopes) something to satisfy the buyer, and ultimately its shareholders. However, the supplier also has various claimants for shares of its slice, and again its intention is to have something left over to fund its own future growth and satisfy its shareholders.

There are two ways in which the supplier can gain more from the relationship. The first is to secure a larger slice of the pie at the expense of other claimants of the pie, through extending the work it is currently doing into other units of the buyer's organization, or through negotiating an increase in the scope of its activities. The buyer, of course, in supporting such a move would expect to secure a further gain for itself, increasing the size of its slice of pie in the process.

A second way is for the buyer's business to grow – the buyer makes the pie larger. In this scenario, the supplier receives a larger slice of the pie, although it is not increasing its percentage share of the pie. With the traditional and peripheral types of outsourcing identified in Chapter 1, this may be a fairly passive activity by the supplier, responding to the buyer's growth. An increase in the buyer's sales may mean, for example, that orders for components have been increased, that there have been more people using the restaurant facilities, or that additional people have been sent on a particular training programme. The supplier has to keep its promises, and is likely to retain contracts if it performs somewhat better than expected, but at best the supplier is only an enabling factor for the buyer.

The critical and strategic types of outsourcing (see Figure 1.1 and Figure 2.1) offer the best chance of developing a win–win situation. Here there are many situations in which the supplier can help the buyer to grow the supplier's own business, and often situations develop in which both can end up with more pie.

Unfortunately, there are other situations in which the pie shrinks, either the buyer's share of the pie is decreased, or the supplier finds that its claimants gobble up much or all of its slice, meaning that it has no net gain from the contract. Under these circumstances, one party may lose while the other wins, or sometimes both may lose. Such situations may come about because of poor strategies, or changes to market conditions, but may sometimes occur because one party puts pressure on the other to give it a bit more of the pie.

There is one complicating factor for suppliers that increases in significance the closer we move to the strategic end of the outsourcing spectrum. Many of the critical and strategic types of contracts run for several years, involve heavy bidding costs followed by capital expenditure and also entail high initial costs. This situation brings cash flow into the picture and, more specifically, discounted cash flow. Large projects may have a negative net present value for several of the early years and, in non-discounted terms, may require the availability of significant financial resources to maintain liquidity. They may even make a loss in accounting terms in the early years. Therefore, the view of the pie has to go beyond the immediate accounting year.

How good are we at making larger pies?

Well, sometimes pies shrink . . .

> While outsourcing is a rapidly growing part of the industrial scene, survey evidence indicates that the results are often disappointing. Surveys by Lonsdale (1999) and Sauer and Willcocks (2000) conclude that a minority of outsourcing deals are successful. Instances are common in which outsourcing arrangements have been reversed in favour of in-house supply. Such instances include the experience of higher costs following outsourcing (Harley Davidson), lower quality of manufactured products (Games Workshop) and the failure to recognise the criticality and differentiated nature of key IT functions (East Midland Electricity). (Jennings, 2002)

The fact that some buyers are not getting what they require from an outsourcing arrangement is not necessarily the fault of the suppliers. We have already shown that there is a great deal that both parties have to attend to if outsourcing is to work.

Suppliers too can find that nothing is left for them from their slice of the pie. Doig *et al.* (2001, pp. 28–29) cite the situation in the US automotive industry in which there has been a considerable increase in outsourcing, necessitating investment by the suppliers and exposing them to more risk, which has been accompanied by continual demands for lower prices from the powerful buyers. Of course, the OEMs in the automotive industry have faced profitability problems. However, by aggressively cracking the whip over their suppliers, the OEMs have reduced the suppliers' margins so severely that they are cutting their investments in innovation and quality with potential repercussions for the OEMs as in the case of Firestone tyre failure problems. As a consequence of these unprofitable partnerships, it has been suggested that bankruptcies and industry exits may create challenges for the OEMs that could even lead them back into manufacturing once again (Doig *et al.*, 2001, p. 29).

In an earlier chapter we mentioned EDS in conjunction with the risks suppliers take when a long-term contract runs into problems. EDS had been the leading supplier of IT services to the public and private sectors. In September 2002 it issued a profits warning, which led to a reduction of two-thirds of its market value by early October. The chief executive, Dick Brown, stated that EDS would focus its new business on contracts that 'produce more near term revenue, earnings and cash flow'. Hopkins (2002), the source of this information, observed:

> Long-term contracts, such as the £350 million a year deal EDS has with the Inland Revenue, typically take more time to generate positive cash flow. The bidding process for such deals also often takes several months or even years, costing each bidder tens of millions of pounds.

The comment refers to the UK Inland Revenue department. At that time EDS had many large government contracts in the UK, and was believed to have a 12-year £2.1 billion deal with Rolls-Royce, as well as many worth more than £100 million.

EDS built its enormous outsourcing supply business on a long-established IT platform. By contrast, W. T. Atkins, originally an engineering consultancy and a well-respected brand, made its move into the IT outsourcing business based on a somewhat wobblier platform of experience. A profits warning in early October 2002 caused its share price to fall by nearly 75%. Jameson (2002) commented:

> Observers believe Atkins' problems at Southwark are only a fraction of the difficulties caused by the introduction of a disastrous IT investment. Atkins' debt has spiralled to £120 million just as it must find £70 million, more than its stock market value, to invest in the London Underground Public Private Partnership.

Southwark is a London borough and the £100 million contract for educational IT services included 104 schools. Problems included the payment of teachers' salaries, the handling of pension contributions and the payment of suppliers. The issue is not so much what went wrong, but the costs of setting it all right. According to another report (Simpkins, 2002) there were more problems disclosed than just the profits warning:

> It also disclosed a £6.1 million exceptional charge for installing a centralised computer system in Worcester. The Worcester system was designed not only to handle all billing activity from Atkins' 12 divisions operating out of more than 170 offices worldwide, it was also supposed to be a showcase for its skills and would handle clients' outsourced accounting.
>
> The trouble is the system simply wasn't working and insiders estimate that invoices for about £20 million of bills were not sent out.

These few examples illustrate some of the ways in which the pie may shrink, or the slices left for the supplier or the buyer may be inadequate. Some problems are no doubt avoidable, but whatever the cause, outsourcing can only succeed if both parties feel that they are gaining.

But sometimes pies expand...

A recent announcement shows one way of thinking in a partnership relationship. In October 2002 IBM won a $1.1 billion 10-year contract with the retailer Boots. According to the announcement, 'IBM will manage the retailer's IT infrastructure, provide database management and applications maintenance for its loyalty card programme and also deploy and manage new point-of-sale systems in 1,600 stores'. It was announced that some 400 Boots employees would transfer to IBM. A somewhat novel twist to this example was Boots' stated intention to reinvest the savings from this part of the contract in new technologies. The $200 million in estimated savings were to be used in conjunction with IBM at an innovation centre to be established in Nottingham. Through using the initial benefits of the outsourcing to help create a larger pie for the buyer (Boots) from which the seller (IBM) will obtain a larger slice of the pie. Cost reduction is the driver, but it is not an end in itself.

Doig *et al.* (2001, p. 36) give one example of how a buyer of outsourcing has been changing its business:

> Sony, for instance, has eliminated 11 of its 70 plants, plans to cut 4 more by 2003, and now outsources its original PlayStation to companies in China. Newly created manufacturing subsidiaries will oversee its remaining facilities, where novel, strategically important products such as its PlayStation 2 will be made. Sony expects this strategy to bring its current 5.5 percent return on equity closer to the 15 percent and more achieved by US technology competitors.

To provide a more comprehensive picture of outsourcing profitability we will look specifically at strategies for sellers and for buyers.

How sellers can make the pie larger

The seller of outsourcing solutions has opportunities to obtain a larger slice of the pie and also to work with the buyer to make a larger pie. Four specific observations arising from the outsourcing research project conducted by Copenhagen Business School and Oxford Research A/S led to suggestions that they could contribute to enhanced profitability from the provision of outsourcing solutions. The suggestions are summarized below:

1. *Develop an understanding of customers' core competencies.* A good understanding of the customer's core competencies requires that the seller have a thorough and in-depth understanding of the customer's activity cycle. Also valuable are the general competitive dynamics of the customer's industry and the forces driving change in this industry. Without this understanding it is difficult for sellers to position their offerings.
2. *Assist customers to support/upgrade their core competencies.* Because of the intimate relationship between the competitiveness of sellers and buyers, it is valuable for the seller to identify ways to enhance the buyer's core competencies in order to position the buyer more competitively.
3. *Complement customers' core competencies for strategic fit.* Sellers should be able to complement the buyer's core competencies in such a way as to create a strategic fit between the core competencies of the two organizations. To do so allows for much more dynamic development of seller's offerings, which often will have to be tailored individually for each buyer.

4. *Develop the capacity to manage and operate in a network.* With the increasing blurring of the traditional boundaries between buyers and sellers it appears that networking capabilities are of ever greater value in managing interfirm relationships. As sellers move from offering traditional products and services to total solutions and facilities management contracts, they begin the process of reinventing their organizations and perhaps even engage in some outsourcing themselves to better meet buyer requirements.

These four areas of relational competence may facilitate the profitable delivery of outsourced services and, in so doing, can be said to help sellers to make larger pies.

How buyers can make the pie larger

The buyer of outsourcing solutions has opportunities to get a larger slice of the pie and to work with the seller of the outsourced solution to make a larger pie. The key to successful outsourcing – the essential skills for making outsourcing decisions, for managing outsourcing contracts and for providing the necessary oversight to the outsourcing relationships – revolves around a set of leadership capabilities (Useem and Harder, 2000). These leadership capabilities were identified in the course of a large-scale study that involved in-depth interviews with 54 senior managers of 25 large American and international firms. Each of the four principal leadership skills identified was not unique to the practice of outsourcing, but the study found that the combination of these four skills was critical to the 'lateral leadership' found to be essential for working effectively in outward interfirm relationships as opposed to the downward relationships within a company. The key elements of effective outsourcing leadership are summarized below:

1. *Think strategically about outsourcing decisions.*
    Within the outsourcing framework it is essential to determine whether to outsource and how to do so in order to improve competitive advantage. The literature does contain some valuable tools to help with this complex decision-making process. Some key examples are the work of Insinga and Werle (2000) that focuses on linking outsourcing to business strategy in order to overcome operational level outsourcing pitfalls, and the work of Quinn and Hilmer (1994) that focuses on identifying the company's main core competences and outsourcing strategically many other activities taking relative costs and risks into account.

2. *Broker external and internal outsourcing deals simultaneously.*
    It is essential to ensure that the outsourcing deals made provide the most appropriate services from external providers and provide the most effective use of these services by internal users within the company.

3. *Govern partnership relationships adeptly.*
    Following the above two steps it is then necessary to oversee the governance of the partnership to ensure that the relationship continues to operate effectively.

4. *Spearhead change to overcome employee resistance.*
    Employee resistance to outsourcing should be anticipated and leadership strategies to manage the change effectively often require forceful spearheading.

These four areas of lateral leadership competence in combination can help buyers to gain greatest value from outsourced service providers and thereby facilitate the creation of larger pies.

In the final analysis

The new relationship opportunities that are a central theme in profitable business outsourcing are increasingly influenced by the impacts of internationalization. Managing globally based relationships – whether it be call centres in India, repair and service centres in Eastern Europe, manufacturing centres in Mexico, or one of the many other international outsourcing options available – adds a further level of complexity to successful outsourcing. The challenges associated with cross-cultural management cannot be underestimated or dismissed as trivial matters.

This book was designed to address one major issue – Can money be made from the new relationship opportunities? There is a range of management issues implicated in the response to this question. The various chapters of the book have focused on key topics such as approaches to opportunity identification, marketing and sales force management, buyer/supplier relationships, pricing, human resource transitions, IT solutions, quality standards and increased profitability. We have attempted to uncover constructive 'keys to success', primarily based on the findings of a three-year outsourcing research project carried out in Copenhagen along with some results from other international studies. To consider the profitability question we will look at one final example, the case of a medical billing service for doctors aptly named Claimpower, Inc. (Karmin, 2004).

The Claimpower story

This example illustrates both seller perspectives and buyer perspectives and presents the small business viewpoint rather than that of the global giants so often featured in the outsourcing literature.

Claimpower provides a service originally developed to help New Jersey doctors file medical insurance claims (Karmin, 2004). In 1985 the current owner of the company took over the business from its founder for whom he had designed a software system for medical claim processing. Today the owner runs the business together with his wife. Initially he employed part-time workers in New Jersey to help with the data entry.

When the business owner decided to expand the business in 2001 and had already concluded that it would be too expensive to take on additional employees in New Jersey, he returned to his native India and recruited a manager and two workers for the high volume of largely predictable and repetitive data entry tasks – inputting figures on a computer, printing out forms and proof-reading them, stuffing envelopes and telephoning the American insurance companies with follow-up questions. The salaries for the Indian workers range from $133 to $663 per month, good salaries by local standards. As a result of his lower data entry costs, he was able to charge significantly less than his competitors for his billing services, thereby helping to expand his business from 10 to 41 clients in a two-year period and freeing up his time to offer clients specialized attention. The next business step for Claimpower is to expand nationally with a target of 500 doctors nationwide after hiring of a sales team to recruit clients and new managers to work with doctors along with an additional 30 staff in India.

One of the outsourcing lessons that this owner learned early on involved personnel difficulties – the manager in India did not understand the business and was not able to train the two workers effectively, a situation that led to claim-processing errors. In 2002 the owner decided to leave his position as a Wall Street programmer and devote himself full time to his small business. He went to India once again and found a new manager who he personally trained and then assisted to recruit four data processors who he also personally trained. He now has 30 Indian personnel.

The performance of Claimpower has been exemplary: with commissions on average of 5% of the amounts collected from insurers one doctor reported that Claimpower's fees were less than half the fees charged by his previous billing service that made far too many mistakes! The quality of the Claimpower service allows doctors to focus on their patients rather than office administration matters.

What can we learn from this example? The Claimpower experience of sourcing decisions – as an outsourcing solution buyer of data entry services from Indian workers and as an outsourcing solution seller of medical billing services to American doctors – offers some useful insights on how buyers and sellers can get larger slices of the pie and how buyers and sellers can make the pie larger. From the seller perspective Claimpower increases the size of its slice of pie through its lower commissions and its accurate claim processing at the expense of its competitors. When the medical practices of its buyers grow, they make the pie larger and Claimpower's slice along with it. From the buyer perspective Claimpower has made its pie larger through the growth of its business with the consequence that it can recruit more Indian personnel for data entry and more American personnel for marketing and business development. The planned expansion of the business that becomes possible with specialized marketing and business development personnel and also increased data entry capacity mean that the company has the potential to create a much larger pie.

Summary

The many examples of sourcing decisions used in this and the previous eight chapters are intended to provide useful illustrations of the potential windfalls and the potential pitfalls from the seller perspective. Observations on buyer perspectives are also included as these illustrate the impact of seller decisions. In the final analysis profitable business outsourcing requires that the perspectives of both the seller and the buyer be taken into account.

From the seller perspective *relational management skills* play a key role in profitable business outsourcing – understanding buyers' core competencies in a broader industry context, supporting/upgrading these competencies and complementing them to create a strategic fit between the organizations as well as developing networking capabilities – are valuable strategies for making the outsourcing pie larger.

From the buyer perspective *lateral leadership skills* play a key role in profitable business outsourcing – the combination of thinking strategically, making external and internal deals simultaneously, governing partnership relationships adeptly and spearheading change to overcome employee resistance – are, when taken collectively, a valuable strategy for making the outsourcing pie larger.

Can money be made from the new relationship opportunities? Specific skills help considerably to determine the answer to this question.

References

Doig, S. J., Ritter, R. C., Speckhals, K. and Woolson, D. 2001. Has outsourcing gone too far? *McKinsey Quarterly*, No. 4.

Hopkins, N. 2002. EDS think again about large-scale contracts, *The Times*, 2 October.

Insigna, R. C. and Werle, M. J. 2000. Linking outsourcing to business strategy, *Academy of Management Executive*, Vol. 14, No. 4, pp. 58–70.

Jameson, A. 2002. Atkins blunder hits teacher pay, *The Times*, 5 October.

Jennings, D. 2002. Outsourcing: motives and policy, *Journal of Professional HRM*, January.

Karmin, C. 2004. 'Offshoring' by small businesses may create jobs in the U.S., *The Wall Street Journal*, 16 March.

Lonsdale, C. 1999. Effectively managing vertical supply relationships: A risk management model for outsourcing, *Supply Chain Management*, Vol. 4, No. 4.

Quinn, J. B. and Hilmer, F. G. 1994. Strategic outsourcing, *MIT Sloan Management Review*, Summer, pp. 43–55.

Sauer, C. and Willcocks, L. 2000. High risks and hidden costs in IT outsourcing, *Financial Times*, 23 May.

Simpkins, E. 2002. Why Trinity Mirror won't pay the Piper, *Sunday Telegraph*, 6 October.

Useem, M. and Harder, J. 2000. Leading laterally in company outsourcing, *Sloan Management Review*, Winter, pp. 25–36.

Index

Index compiled by Annette Musker